Richard Hünecke / Bob Shell

Olympus IS-2, IS-3 and IS-10

Magic Lantern Guides
Proof of Purchase
Olympus IS-2, IS-3
and IS-10

Richard Hünecke / Bob Shell

OLYMPUS

iS-2 iS-3

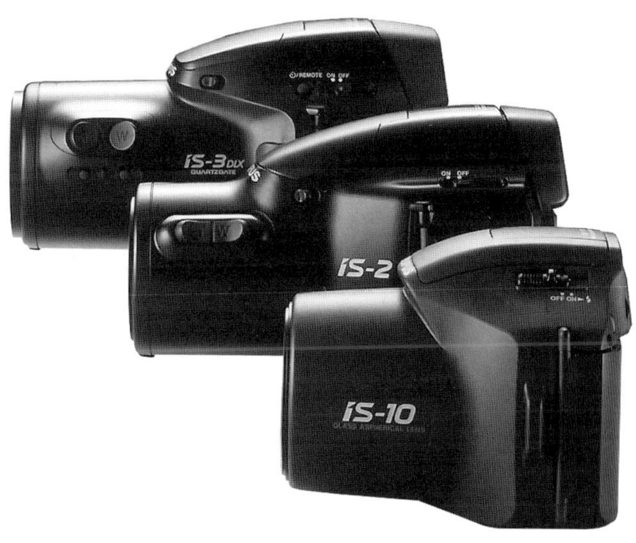

Laterna magica

Magic Lantern Guide to
Olympus IS-2, IS-3, IS-10

A Laterna magica® book

First Edition, August 1994
Published in the United States of America by
Silver Pixel Press
Divison of
The Saunders Group
21 Jet View Drive
Rochester, NY 14624

Based on the German editions *Olympus IS-2000*
and *Olympus IS-3000* by Richard Hünecke
Translated by Bob Shell and Phyllis M. Riefler-Bonham
Edited by Bob Shell
Editorial Assistant: Mimi Netzel
Production Coordinator: Marti Saltzman

Printed in Germany by Kösel GmbH, Kempten

ISBN 1-883403-05-7

 The editor acknowledges Bryant Kling and Bill Schoonmaker, both of Olympus America Inc., for their help on this book. Without their enthusiastic support, this book would not have been possible. A special thank you must go to Art Evans who wrote the chapter on the Olympus G40 flash and provided useful suggestions on the book.

Contents

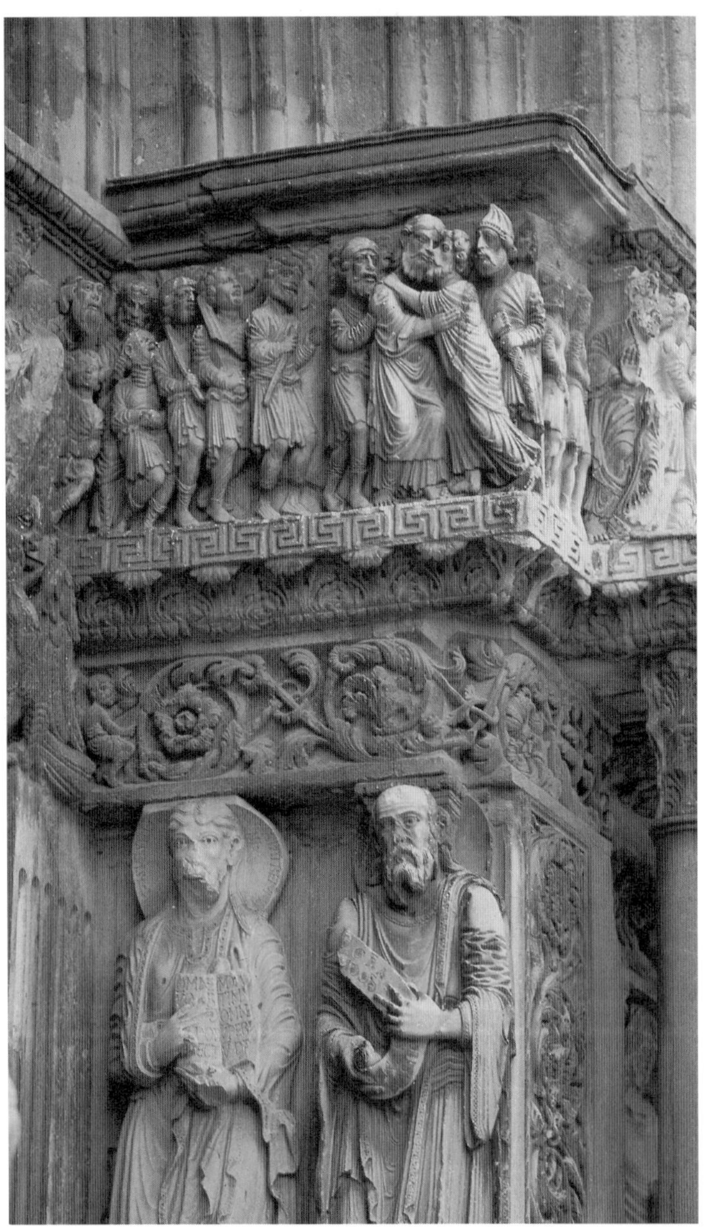

Introduction: The IS Concept

At the present time, the Olympus IS-series is comprised of four cameras: the IS-1, IS-2, IS-3, and IS-10 (or IS-1000, IS-2000, IS-3000 and IS-100, depending on the country of sale). Essentially they are identical cameras with different model designations. However, there are a few exceptions which are noted in the sections specific to the feature differences. To keep this text from becoming too cumbersome, I have used the shorter USA model designations throughout, only mentioning the European designations when the information applies to them exclusively. Also, since the instruction manuals which Olympus provides with the IS cameras are excellent and easy to understand, this text will concentrate on how the camera features can be applied for the best possible results.

The IS-series cameras are self-contained ZLRs (zoom lens reflex) encased in a compact and ergonomic housing with a permanently attached zoom lens. The IS cameras are remarkably capable cameras, offering in one compact unit all of the features that most photographers will ever need. Even though the lenses are not extremely fast, they are fast enough for modern films in most situations, and the built-in flash units extend that range when there is insufficient ambient light for normal photography.

Overall, the Olympus IS cameras are similar and the same operational sequences apply to all four. For this reason I have treated them as the same in the general discussions of photographic technique in this book and have discussed them individually in separate short sections so that the reader will be familiar with the differences. At the time of writing, the IS-2, IS-3 and IS-10 are current models, and the IS-1 has been discontinued. Essentially, the IS-2 is an updated and improved IS-1.

The compact, versatile design of the IS-series cameras makes them perfect for travel photography. The built-in flash and zoom lens allow you to capture everything from landscapes to architectural details without packing a lot of gear.

When the IS-1 was first introduced, I borrowed one from Olympus and took it with me as a second camera on several photographic assignments. I used it to shoot most of the things I was photographing with my own SLR and its array of interchangeable lenses. I was very pleased with the ease of operation of the IS-1, and quickly realized that it could do just about anything I would usually do on a photo assignment. Its only limitations were lack of an extremely wide-angle lens and a longer telephoto lens. When I examined the processed transparencies on my light box, it was difficult to tell which had been taken with which camera system. I know you have heard through advertising that the lenses on the IS cameras are something special, and this is factual, not advertising hype. Olympus uses glass and mechanical elements of the highest quality in the IS lenses. Images shot with the three IS cameras are among the sharpest and have the best contrast of any in my collection of transparencies. They are up to anyone's standards of professional quality.

Bob Shell
Radford, VA
May 1994

Photographs taken using the telephoto lens setting make animals at the zoo seem close enough to touch. 

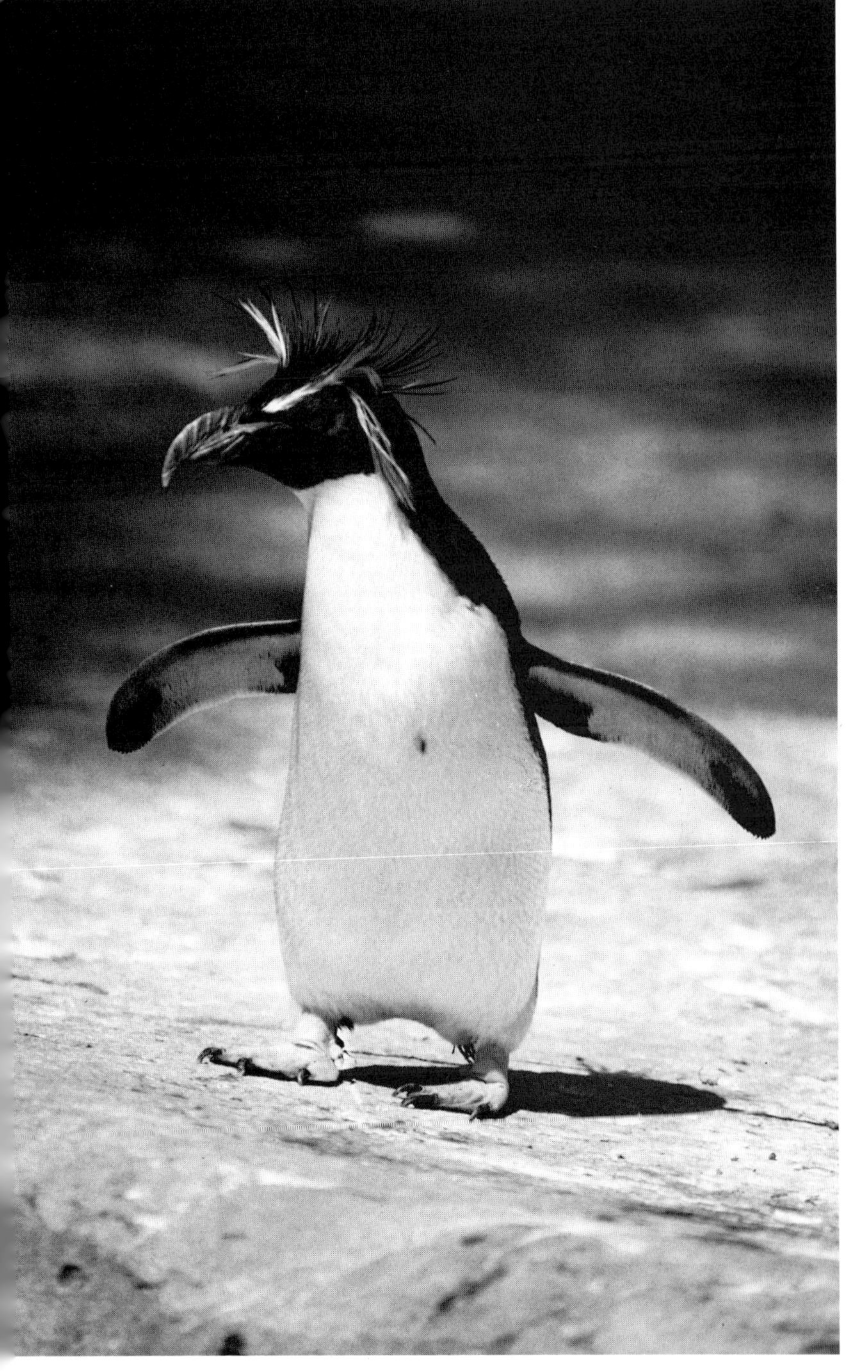

Olympus IS Cameras

General Specifications

All the IS-series cameras are similar in general design, layout and operation. By basic definition, they are SLR (Single Lens Reflex) cameras, meaning a mirror system allows the photographer to see through the same lens that is focusing the image onto the film. Olympus uses the term ZLR, or Zoom Lens Reflex, in reference to the cameras' built-in zoom lens. The cameras are also called "bridge cameras" because they span the gap between "point and shoots" and more complex SLR systems with interchangeable lenses and accessories.

The camera body is a composite design made from glass fiber-reinforced resins to be durable and lightweight. Each camera's lens is a sophisticated, multi-element zoom which utilizes optical technology found in lenses of the highest quality. An ED element in the IS-1, IS-2, and IS-3 corrects for chromatic aberration and produces sharper images through the entire range of focal lengths. The zoom lens of the IS-10 has been updated with an aspherical lens element for image clarity and reduced distortion. In addition to creating sharp, clear images, the lens design of the IS series makes them more compact than a conventional SLR camera and zoom lens combination.

All three cameras use an unusual reverse-curl film path. The S-shaped path of the IS-2 and IS-3 and J-shaped path of the IS-10 have allowed Olympus to make each camera much narrower than it could be with a more traditional film path. However, this unusual film path also requires some attention to film loading, particularly if you are used to loading any other type of 35mm camera.

The Olympus IS-3 showing the optical path through the 35-180mm ED lens. Extra Low Dispersion (ED) glass bends the blue and red light so both focus on the same plane. Using ED glass also produces more compact lens designs. The innovative "S-curve" film path is also clearly visible in this cut-away top view.

Glossary

The terms defined here are referred to throughout the text as the various features and functions of the IS-series cameras are explained. They are standard photographic terms which apply to most cameras.

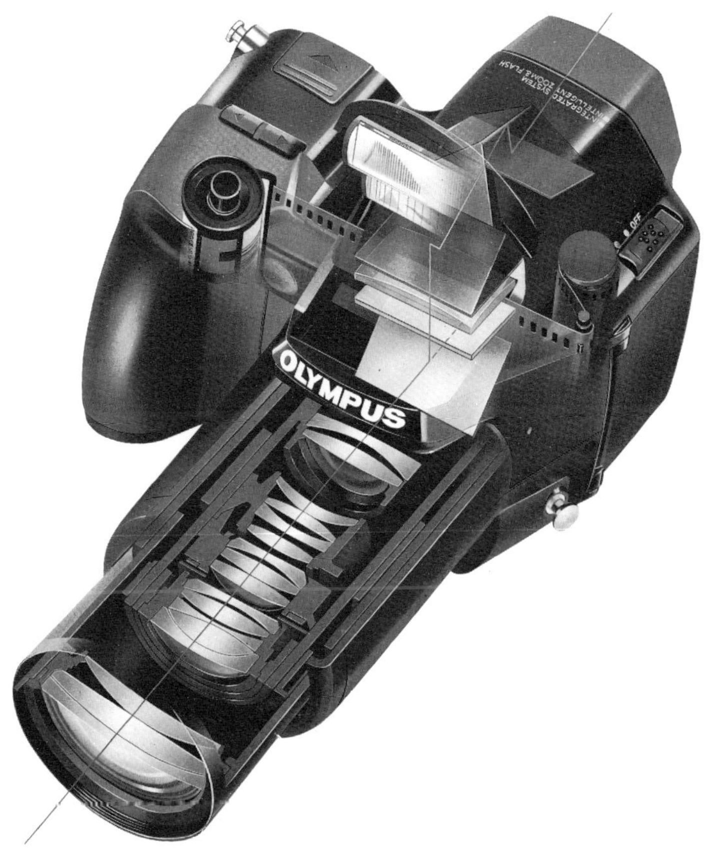

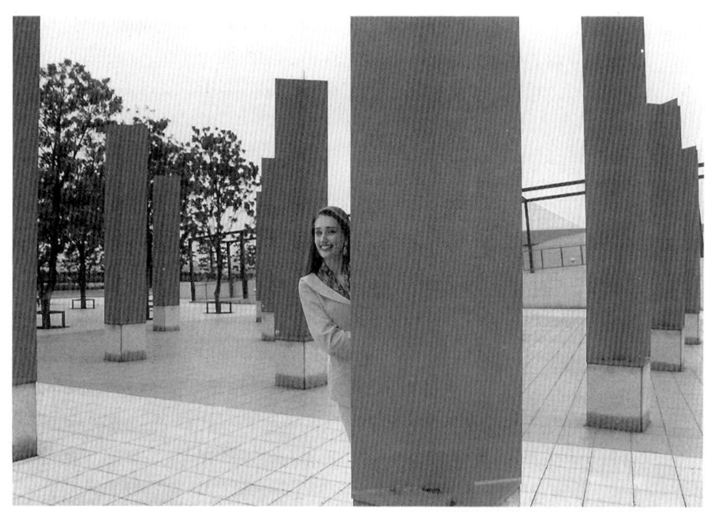

The compositional differences between focal lengths of 110mm (top) and 28mm are apparent in these images. Both photos were taken from the same position with an Olympus IS-10 camera.

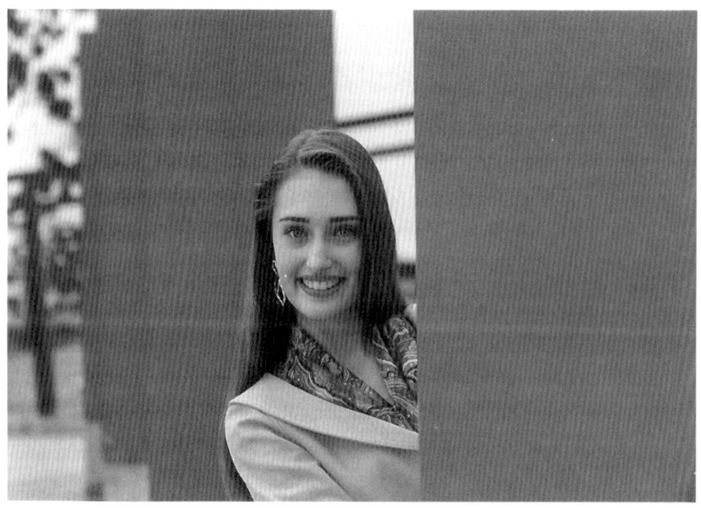

Focal length: The distance from the film plane to the optical center of the lens is the lens' focal length. 50mm is considered a "normal" focal length setting for a 35mm camera because it approximates a person's angle of view. As focal length decreases, the lens' angle of view gets wider. Obviously, this is why a short focal length lens is called a wide-angle lens. As focal length increases, the angle of view gets narrower. Long focal lenses are called telephoto lenses. A lens with a range of possible focal lengths, such as the lens on an IS-series camera, is called a zoom lens.

Aperture: The hole created by the bladed diaphragm near or at the rear of the lens. The aperture is what controls the amount of light that strikes the film. The size of the aperture hole is communicated in f/stops (see below). The larger the diameter of the aperture hole the lower the f/stop number; the smaller the diameter, the higher the f/stop number.

f/stop: In reality, it is a formula for calculating the physical diameter of the aperture (though photographers do not think of it in this way). Knowing the mathematical formula is not necessary for taking photographs though. Aperture and f/stop though technically different terms, are interchanged commonly. What is important is the understanding that they affect exposure and depth of field.

Depth of field: An area of sharpness which falls in front of and behind the subject on which the lens is focused. Generally, depth of field falls 1/3 in front of and 2/3 behind the plane of focus. The depth of this zone of focus is dictated by the combination of the focal length of the lens and the f/stop. A general rule of thumb is the smaller the aperture (i.e. f/22) the greater the depth of field and the larger the aperture (i.e. f/4.5), the narrower the depth of field. If the f/stop remains constant, depth of field increases as focal length decreases.

Contrast: The visual difference in brilliance or brightness between different elements in a scene. These differences are described as highlights and shadows and the difference in properly exposing for these determines the range of contrast in the scene.

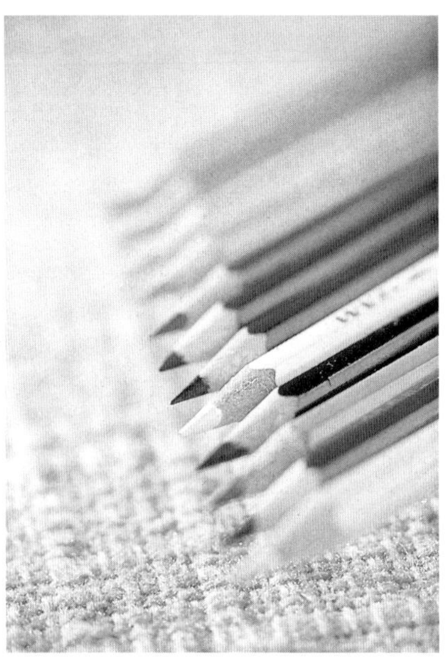

f/5.6

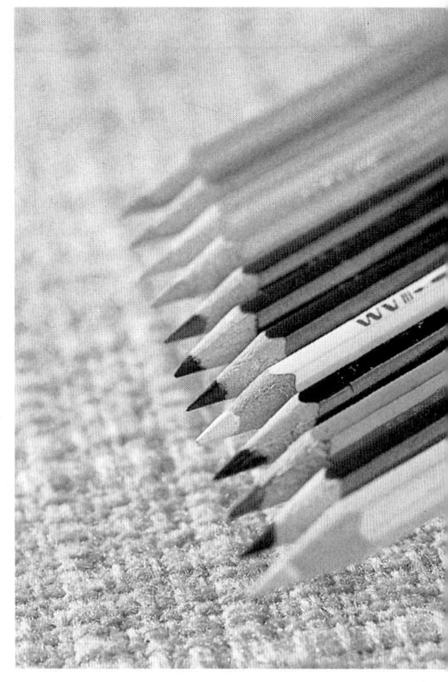

f/1

f/22

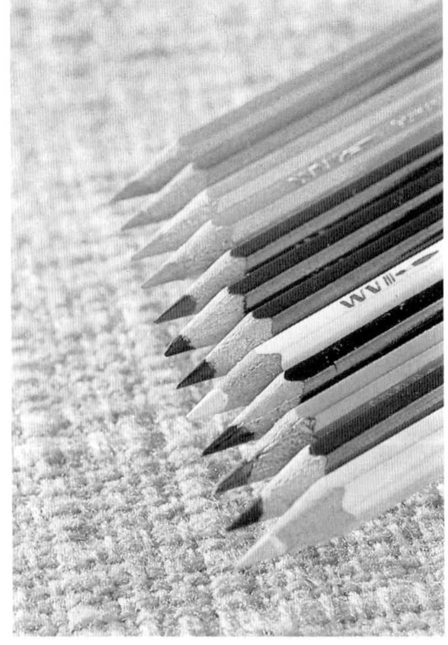

These three photographs illustrate how depth of field changes as the aperture is adjusted. The camera is focused on the white pencil approximately 1/3 of the distance into the image.

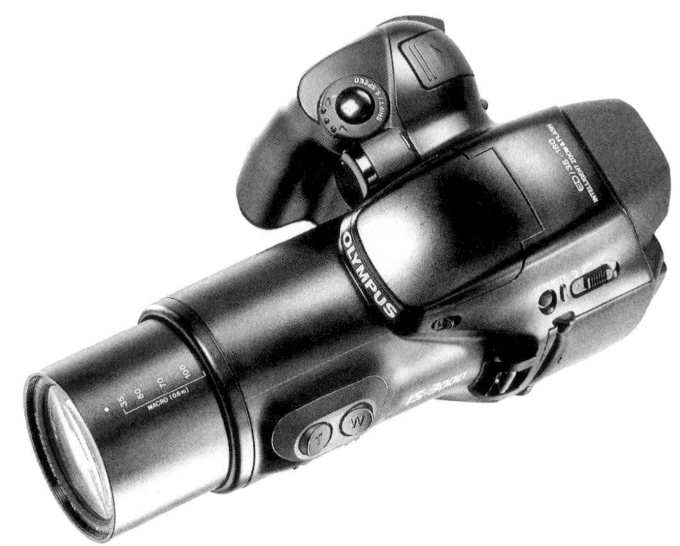

The IS-series cameras are designed to be sleek and easy to handle.

Getting Started

Its ergonomic design makes it almost impossible to hold an IS camera incorrectly. Just curl your right hand around the grip so that your forefinger sits above the shutter release button and use your left hand to support the camera from underneath. Use the thumb of your left hand to operate the lens control buttons of the IS-1, IS-2, and IS-3. For the IS-10, your right thumb controls the zoom buttons located on the upper right corner of the camera back. This gives very steady support and allows you to take pictures without having to move your hands or hunt for controls. For vertical shots, just rotate the camera so that your right hand is on top and your left hand beneath. The camera still operates in the same way.

Batteries

The IS cameras will not operate without fresh batteries. Two 3-volt CR123A or DC123A lithium batteries should be installed in

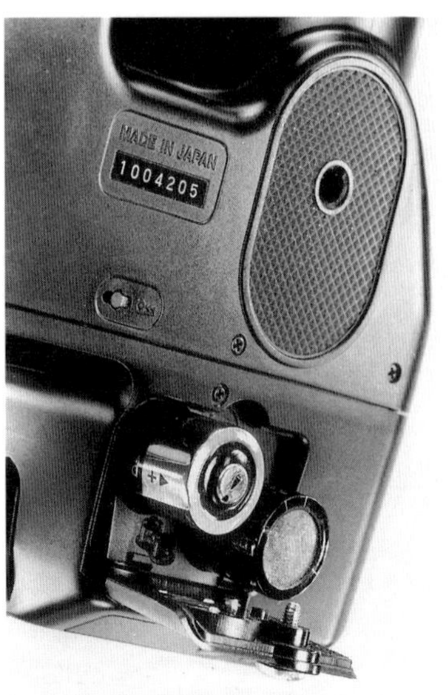

On the underside of the IS-series cameras is the battery compartment. Batteries should be inserted as shown on the battery compartment cover.

the bottom of the camera according to the diagram on the battery compartment cover. The batteries will provide energy for approximately 20 to 25 rolls of 24 exposure film. Battery life is affected by how often the zoom lens and flash are used.

To check the batteries in the IS-2, turn the camera on and then press the Reset button. If the batteries are OK the battery symbol on the LCD display will remain continuous; if it blinks, the batteries should be replaced.

With the IS-3, the two buttons on the left side of the liquid crystal display (MODE and +/-) should be pressed simultaneously. If the battery is low, the battery symbol will blink or appear half empty. In either case, replace the batteries.

The IS-10 performs an automatic battery check when the camera is switched on. The battery symbol appears in the upper right corner of the LCD panel. If the outline of the battery appears full, the battery is good. If the outline appears half full or blinks, the battery needs to be replaced.

It is important to use good batteries at all times with the IS cameras. Since cold temperatures affect battery response, a spare set should be carried inside a shirt pocket if shooting in cold weather conditions for long periods of time. Lithium batteries have a very long "shelf-life," making it convenient to keep a spare set on hand at all times.

Setting the Film Speed

The IS-series cameras have internal sensors in the film cassette chamber which recognize a film's DX coding and automatically set the ISO or film speed. The IS-1 and IS-2 have nine possible settings consisting of the most popular speeds. The IS-10 has over a dozen ISO settings and the IS-3 recognizes film speeds from 25-5000 in 1/3 stop increments. Although it is unlikely, if a film speed is used that is not on the camera's scale, the closest lower ISO will be set. If non-DX coded films are used, the camera will automatically set to ISO 32.

Loading the Film

To open the back for film loading, slide the recessed back cover release upward and swing the back open. Note that it has a support strut to keep it from opening too far. Never try to open it wider than 45 degrees or you will damage the camera. After the back is opened, align the film cassette with the protruding end of the film spool facing toward the top of the camera and slip it into the film chamber. Do this by putting the bottom of the cassette in first and then swinging the top part down into the film chamber. Press to make sure that it is all the way in. The film leader should then lie across the film rails and aperture inside the camera. Make sure that the end of the film leader extends to the left at least as far as the orange-colored film guide. If not, pull a little more film out of the cassette until it reaches, but not enough to extend past the camera back hinge. Carefully slip the top edge of the film under the lip of the orange-colored film guide.

It is vitally important during film loading to remember that the camera shutter is exposed when the camera back is open and that it is extremely fragile. Do not touch or press against the shutter when loading the film. If you need to clean dust from inside the camera do so only with a soft brush made for the purpose and a stream of air from a squeeze-bulb type of blower (I favor the common ear syringe available from most pharmacies). I do not recommend the compressed "canned air" for this, as the bursts of air may be too powerful and may damage the shutter blades.

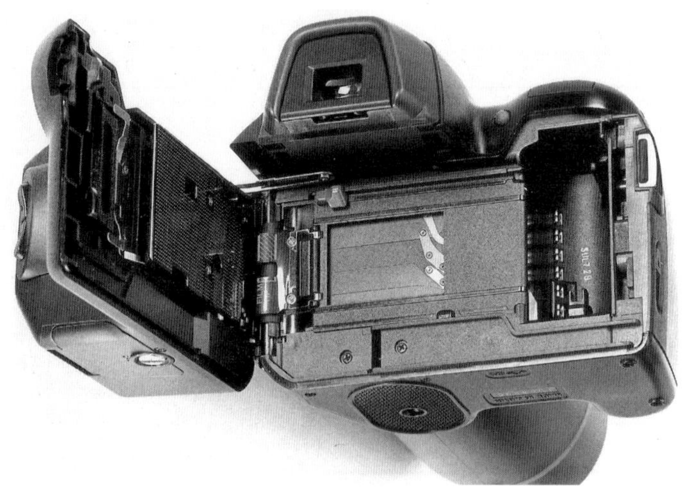

The S-Path Film System
Olympus has designed the IS-1, -2 and -3 cameras with an innovative film path that makes them more sleek than other 35mm SLR cameras. The film cassette sits in the handgrip and is guided from right to left into the thick rear wall following an S-shaped path. The DX coding sensors are visible in the film cassette chamber.

Once the film has been placed as directed, close the back of the camera. If the camera is not switched on, do so now. The film will advance into the "S"-shaped film chamber of the IS-2 and IS-3 with each new shot. This prevents exposed film from being ruined if the camera back is opened accidentally. If an E blinks on the exposure counter on the LCD panel instead of the number 1, you must open the back and reload the film. This E indicates that the film did not advance for some reason.

In most cases, once you have loaded a roll of film, you will use the entire roll. However, it sometimes happens that you will want to have a roll of film processed before you have used up all the frames. You can start the rewind motor and rewind the film at any time on any of the IS cameras by pressing the recessed film rewind button located on the back of the IS-2 and on the bottom of the IS-3 and IS-10.

Now that you have gotten this far in the book, load up your camera with your favorite film and start taking pictures. This basic information will get you started, and you can learn the rest of the detailed information in the book as you progress in your understanding of photography.

Autofocus

Autofocus is a wonderful convenience, but it is not foolproof. The photographer needs to know the limitations of his equipment. Olympus IS-series cameras use TTL phase-difference detection in their focusing systems. A horizontal array sensor focuses the lens by analyzing the perpendicular edge contrast of a subject. The vast majority of subjects have enough tone variation and texture to allow for trouble-free autofocus operation. However, images with low contrast, such as a smooth wall, can present a problem, as can lines which run parallel to the horizontal array sensor. For example, in the horizontal position, the camera may have trouble focusing on venetian blinds. Although autofocus works best when operated in strong light, the IS-series cameras have an infrared AF illuminator which assists the autofocus system automatically in low light situations.

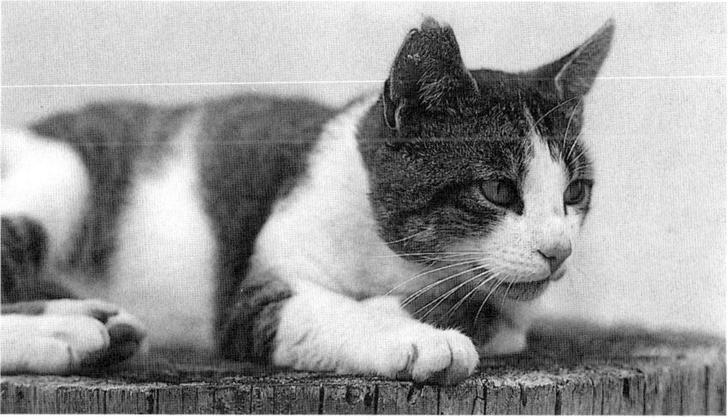

The cat's face was centered in the viewfinder and autofocus was activated. Then to keep this area sharp while the photograph was recomposed, focus lock was engaged by keeping the shutter release partially depressed.

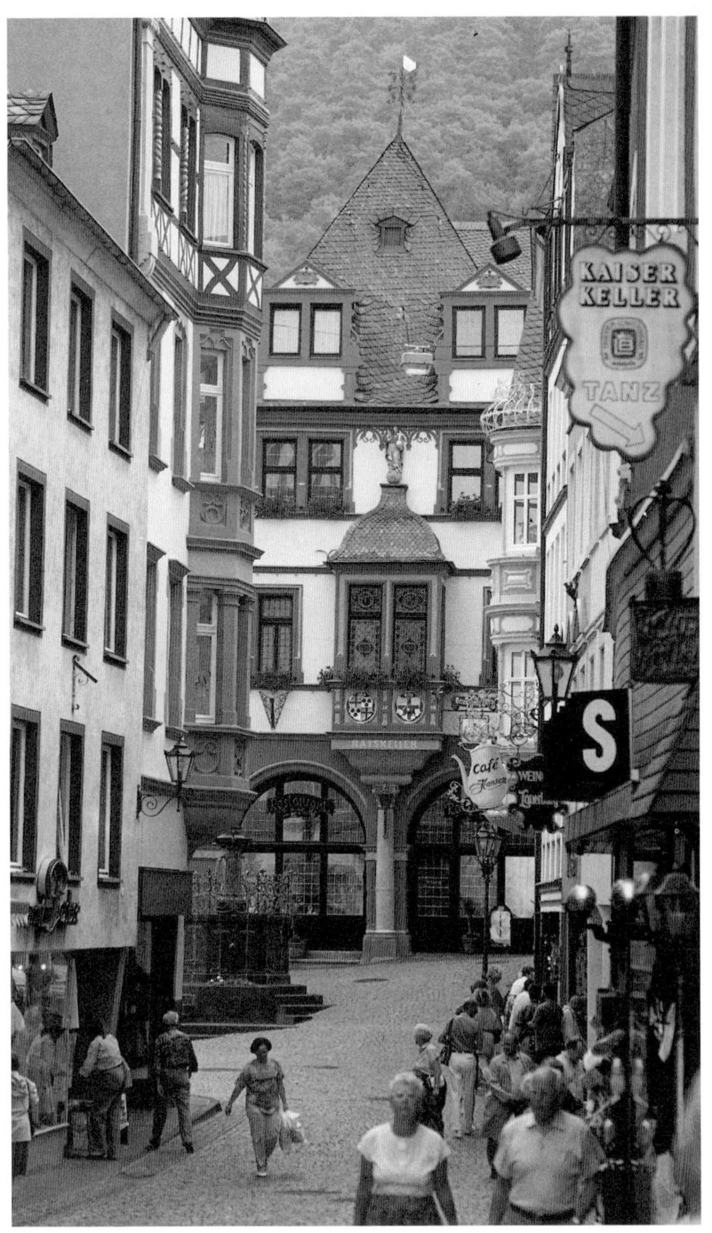
KAISER
KELLER
TANZ
S
Café
WEIN

Note: *Some filters may cause autofocus problems. Soft-focus filters, linear polarizers and other special effects filters are good examples of optical devices that may cause an autofocus malfunction. A linear polarizer should not be used on an autofocus camera; a circular polarizer will not interfere with the autofocus system.*

Autofocus Lock

What if the object you want to have in focus is not centered in the viewfinder? The IS-series cameras offer an autofocus lock feature. Center the subject in the viewfinder's autofocus frame and gently depress the shutter release button until the focus confirmation light comes on in the viewfinder. Without removing the pressure from the shutter-release button, recompose the image and shoot. This must be done with care; changing the distance between the camera and subject will alter the focus. Depressing the shutter release button completely will fire the camera and not keeping enough pressure on it will release the autofocus lock. It is also important to remember that after you take the picture, the focus is no longer locked. If you would like to take a second photograph of the subject, you must center the subject, focus and compose the shot again. Otherwise, the camera will refocus on whatever is centered in the autofocus bracket. This could cost you precious photographs.

The focus lock feature is also useful for getting sharp photographs in situations that are problematic for the autofocus system. Focus on an alternate object at the same distance as the subject, lock the focus, recompose and shoot. If there are strong horizontal lines causing problems for the autofocus system, turn the camera to the vertical position, lock the focus, recompose and shoot.

Canceling the beep (IS-3 only): Should you want to shoot without calling attention to yourself, the camera's audible "in focus" signal can be silenced. The autofocus indicator light in the viewfinder will still let you know when the image is in focus.

To disengage the audible signal, press the Drive Mode and Flash Mode buttons simultaneously until the camera beeps. After

⇦ **The overcast, diffused light on this narrow city street produced a well-exposed photograph with an excellent tonal range.**

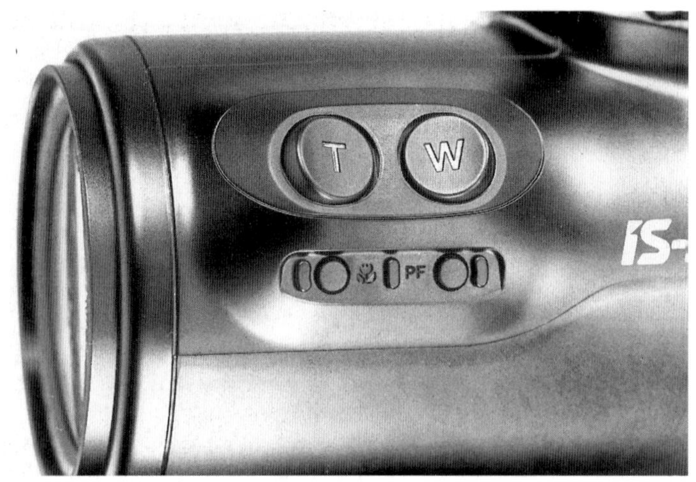

This close-up photo shows the IS-3 zoom lens controls which are also used to focus the lens manually. The button marked PF, for Power Focus, engages and disengages the manual focus control.

that you will only hear the autofocus motor. Pressing the same two buttons will also restore the audible signal.

Manual Focus

Although the IS cameras were designed as autofocus cameras and the autofocus system is among the best yet devised, there are always situations in which autofocus may not offer the best focusing solution. Sometimes it is better to disengage the autofocus system and focus manually. Situations where manual focus may be more effective include very dark subjects, low contrast subjects, subjects with reflective surfaces, strongly backlit subjects or scenes photographed through glass. Because of these situations, Olympus has provided manually operated focus in addition to autofocus on the IS-2 and IS-3 cameras.

The manual focus feature uses the zoom lens' motor drive to focus rather than change the focal length of the lens. For this reason, the lens must first be zoomed to the desired focal length

For off-center subjects, either focus manually on the area you want sharp, or use autofocus lock. 

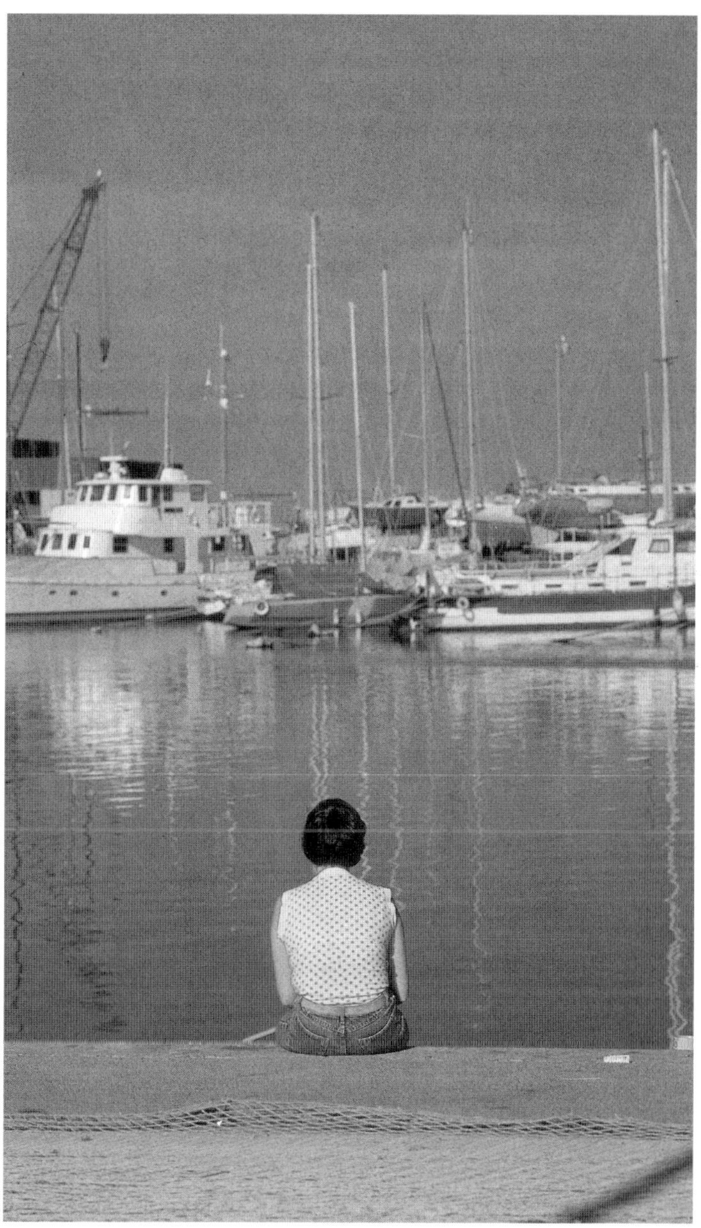

before engaging the manual focus. Olympus refers to their manual focus feature as Power Focus because it uses a motor. To switch to manual focus, set the zoom lens to the desired focal length and then press the PF button. On the IS-2, this is located on the camera back to the upper right of the LCD panel. On the IS-3, it is located below the zoom lens controls on the left side of the camera. Once this button has been pressed, operating the zoom control rocker switch changes the focus. It takes a bit of practice to tell when the image in the viewfinder is sharp, since there are no "in focus" indicators. You may tend to overshoot the point of best focus when you first attempt to use manual focus. But if you work on it a bit, you will get the knack of it.

I can honestly say that in all of my many hours of working with the IS cameras, I have not yet found a subject which required the use of manual focus. In fact, I nearly left it out of this book!

Drive Modes

The IS cameras all have integral, motorized film advance for rapid picture-taking. The IS-10 has only one drive mode, single frame advance. The IS-2 and IS-3 offer a choice of three drive modes: single frame advance, continuous film advance and double exposure.

Single frame advance: For normal operation, the single frame advance is most practical. The shutter release must be pushed for

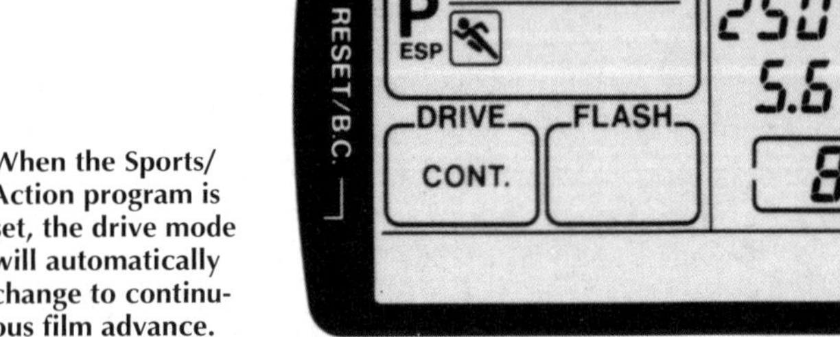

When the Sports/ Action program is set, the drive mode will automatically change to continuous film advance.

each exposure and the film is automatically advanced to the next frame. I would recommend leaving the camera set to "single" for most types of photography. When changing exposure modes, the

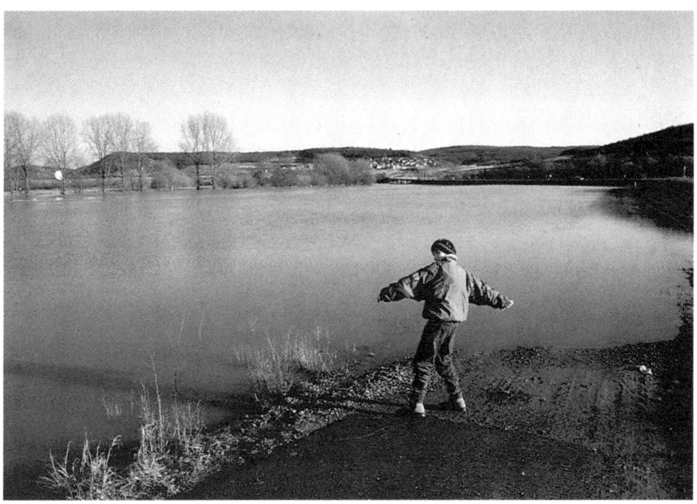

The built-in motor drive is convenient and very fast, allowing you to capture fast action photos. Photo: Herbert Kaspar.

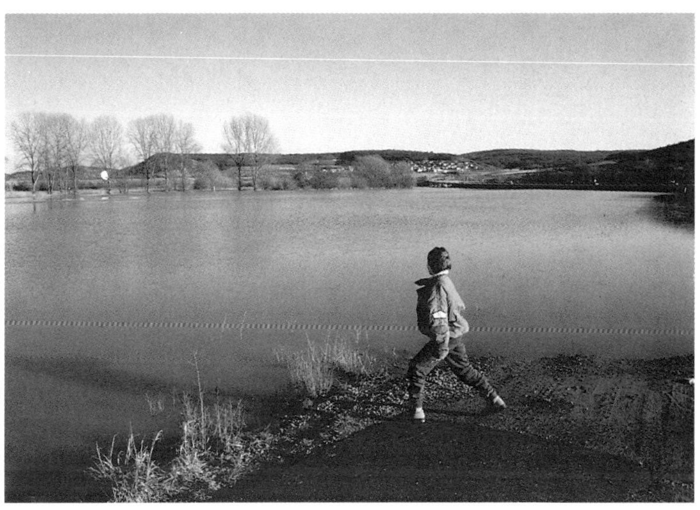

drive mode will automatically reset to single frame advance. The Sports/Action program is the exception; it will automatically select continuous film advance.

Continuous film advance: For photographing really fast action, you may wish to engage the continuous film advance mode. In this setting, the camera will continue to take photographs as long as you maintain pressure on the shutter release button at a maximum rate of about two frames per second. This mode is most suitable if a sequence of shots of a subject in action is desired or to capture a fast moving subject in a specific position.

Double exposure: In this setting, two images can be made on one frame of film for unusual special effects. This is not a true multiple exposure mode because only two exposures may be made. After the second exposure, the camera winds the film to the next frame and automatically switches back to single frame advance mode.

Once the first exposure is made, the double exposure mode cannot be cancelled even by turning off the camera. The photog-

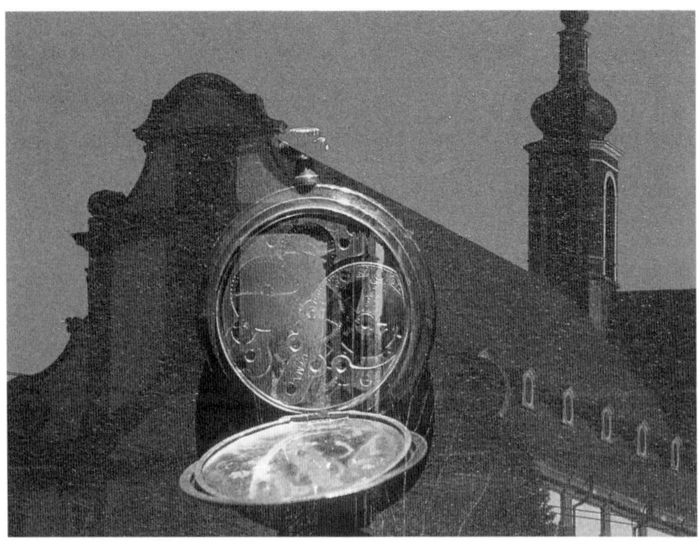

Taken using the double exposure mode, a watch photographed in Macro mode is superimposed on the architecture of a church.

rapher must complete the double exposure sequence. If for some reason a double exposure is not desired, the second exposure could be made with the camera set to Manual focus and the lens cap on. This will satisfy the camera without exposing the film to light.

Setting the Drive Mode (IS-2): The upper left corner of the LCD panel displays the drive mode selected. To change the mode, press the Function button, then press the Drive Mode button until the desired mode appears: S, C, or D.EXP. To lock in the setting, press the Function button or partially depress the shutter release.

Setting the Drive Mode (IS-3): On the left side below the exposure modes, the LCD panel shows the drive mode selected: SINGLE, CONT. or D.EXP. When the Drive Mode button is pressed, all three modes are displayed and a blinking triangle points out the selected mode. Change the mode by holding the Drive button and using either the Shift/Aperture button or Shift/Shutter Speed dial. When the blinking triangle appears next to the appropriate drive mode, release the Drive button.

Self-timer

All the IS cameras have an electronic self-timer with a 12 second delay. This is useful when you want to get into the picture yourself, or when you need the camera to be steady for a shot with a slow shutter speed and do not want to risk camera shake by touching the shutter release.

The camera should be mounted on a tripod or placed on a flat, steady surface. Engage the self-timer by pressing the button marked with the self-timer symbol. The self-timer symbol appears on the LCD panel to confirm activation. Compose and focus on your subject, leaving room for yourself if you plan to jump into the picture. When you press the shutter release button, focus and exposure settings are locked. The self-timer LED/AF illuminator on the front of the camera blinks to countdown operation. After the picture is taken, the self-timer function automatically disengages and must be reset each time for additional use.

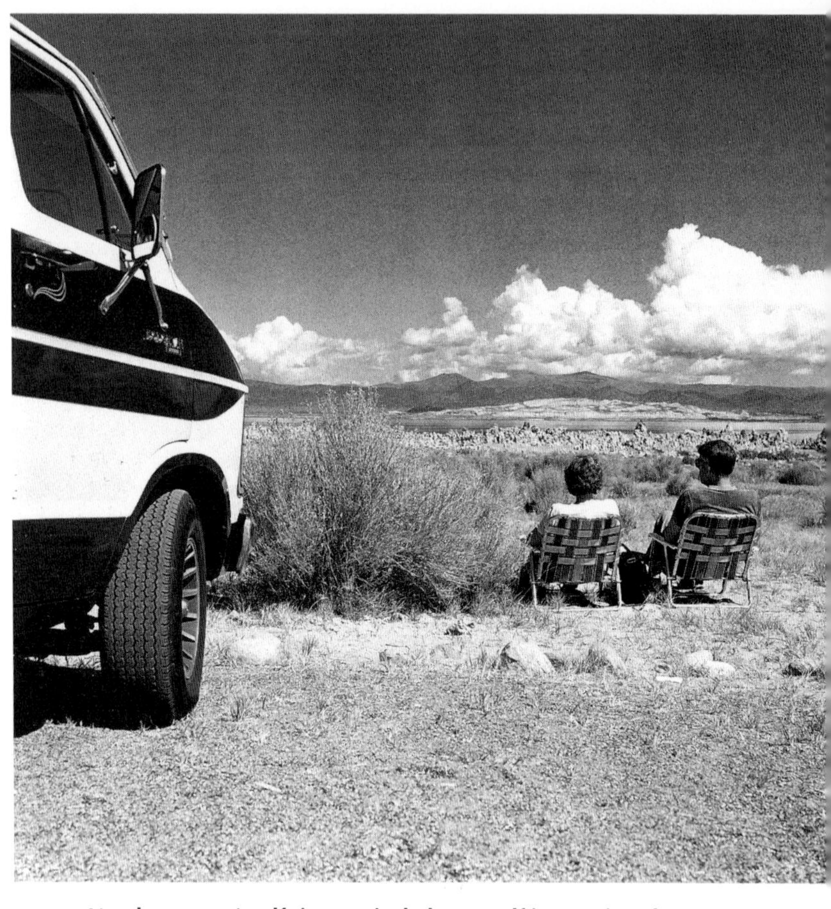

Use the camera's self-timer to include yourself in vacation photos. Photo: Paul Comon.

Caring for Your IS Camera

Cleaning the Camera

Keeping your camera clean will keep it in working order and eliminate unnecessary trips to the camera repair shop. It is a good idea to perform a basic dusting at least once a week even if you do not use the camera heavily. If you do use the camera heavily this should be done more often.

To clean the outside of the camera you will need a blower to provide a stream of pressurized air at a safe pressure and a soft brush. You may use one of the combination blower-brushes sold in photo shops if you like, but I prefer to have the two as separate items. The blower which I prefer does not come from a camera shop at all but from a pharmacy; it is sold as an ear syringe. The ones I like best are large and made from soft natural rubber. The brush I have found best is a number 7 or larger artist's red sable brush, but if you buy one of these do not buy the more expensive grades. You do not need them for this purpose. I use the brush to loosen dust and dirt and then the blower to get rid of it. The outer surfaces of the camera, except for the lens glass and viewfinder glass, may be wiped with one of the silicone impregnated cloths sold in photo shops.

To clean the front surface of the lens, use the brush to loosen any adhering particles and the blower to blow them off. For fingerprints, water spots, etc., you will need to have some lens cleaning tissue and lens cleaning fluid on hand. This is a special tissue which does not produce lint and has no abrasive components. In an emergency, you may use ordinary facial tissue, but be very careful not to scratch the lens. To use the tissue, fold it over several times and then tear it across to produce a fluffy end surface. Wipe the lens gently in a spiral motion, starting at the center and working outwards. Then blow away any debris with the blower. If you have a stubborn spot which this does not remove, dampen a fresh piece of lens tissue (also folded and torn) with just a drop of the lens cleaning fluid and repeat the spiral wiping motion. Repeat this with a new piece of tissue each time until the spot or smear is gone. Never apply the cleaning fluid directly to the lens as it may run down around the edges of the glass and cause damage. Never use any liquid other than lens cleaning fluid or distilled water. Use the same technique to clean the glass in the viewfinder window. You need not exercise quite as much caution here as this glass is much harder than the glass used in the lens.

To clean the interior of the camera, use your brush and blower. Hold the camera pointing upward with the back held open for the final blowing so that any debris will fall downward out of the camera. Be very careful not to touch the shutter while doing this. The shutter curtains are easily damaged and very costly to repair.

Periodically, it is a good idea to wipe down the film pressure plate (the spring loaded plate inside the camera back) and the

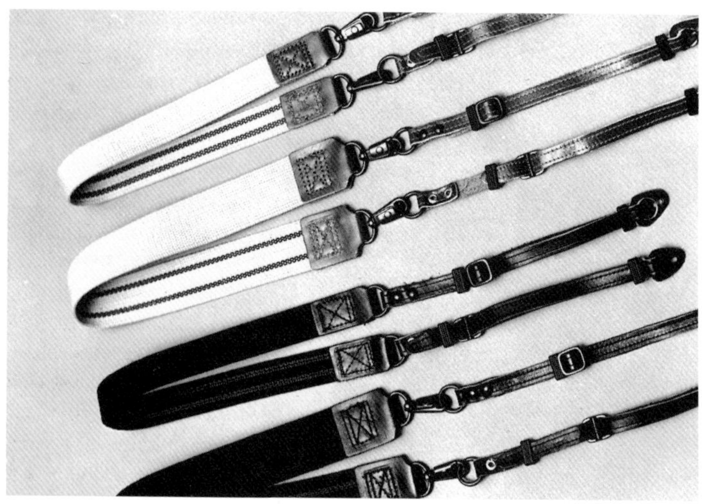

Camera straps come in a variety of styles. The Domke Gripper™ Straps shown here have rubber tracks woven in to keep them from slipping.

film guide rails (the polished surfaces along which the film travels). The best thing to use for this purpose is a soft cloth or cotton swab very slightly dampened with a mixture of distilled water and a little dishwashing detergent. I use a mixture of about two drops in a film can filled with distilled water. This cleans the area and leaves a thin coating of detergent which has anti-static properties. When wiping the film guide rails, exercise extreme caution not to touch or get liquid on the shutter.

Protecting the Camera

Two accessories that every photographer should invest in for the camera's sake are a camera strap and a UV or skylight filter. Wear the strap around your neck when shooting and over your shoulder or across your chest to carry the camera. Do not walk with the camera dangling by the strap. The filters are either clear (UV) or very pale pink (skylight) and simply screw to the front of the lens to protect the front element. Both also filter out UV light which is invisible to the human eye but can reduce contrast and clarity in photographs.

Checking the camera's batteries is a good habit to get into. Batteries can leak, causing expensive problems, and therefore should be inspected every six months. If the camera is not going to be used for a period of a month or more, remove film and batteries from the camera. Do not store batteries with the camera. If batteries are removed from the camera for more than 24 hours while there is film in the camera, the film counter memory will be erased. When batteries are then reinserted, the film will advance three frames and the counter will read "1" instead of the actual exposure number.

Avoid leaving the camera in excessively hot or cold conditions, such as in a car on a summer or winter day. Temperature extremes are detrimental to film as well as the camera and can cause dead batteries, pictures with poor color balance, condensation in the camera, and expansion or contraction of parts.

Under normal use, this is all you should have to do to keep everything in prime operating condition. In unusually dusty environments or at the beach, it is important to keep the camera as clean as possible. Just a few grains of sand can do great damage to the focusing mechanism of the lens. If you must take photos in such dusty or sandy locations, here's a tip I have used. After loading the camera, put it into a medium-sized plastic bag, after first cutting a hole the size of the front of the lens. Hold the bag to the lens with a rubber band, putting the band around the non-moving part of the lens. Allow some of the plastic to extend ahead of the band to form a protective shade for the lens. The bag can then be sealed shut and nothing can get inside. The photographer must still use care to keep grit from getting into the lens, but the bag offers some protection. This same plastic bag trick also works well in wet weather to keep the camera dry. With the IS cameras, all of the normal controls can be operated right through the bag.

Note: *If your camera malfunctions, please do not attempt to fix it yourself. This is a highly advanced machine with sensitive electrical components and the amount ofdamage you could do is likely to increase the ultimate repair bill. The camera should be taken to an authorized Olympus dealer or shipped to the closest Olympus warranty repair station. Remember to include a copy of the camera warranty registration and proof of purchase, if the camera qualifies for warranty service.*

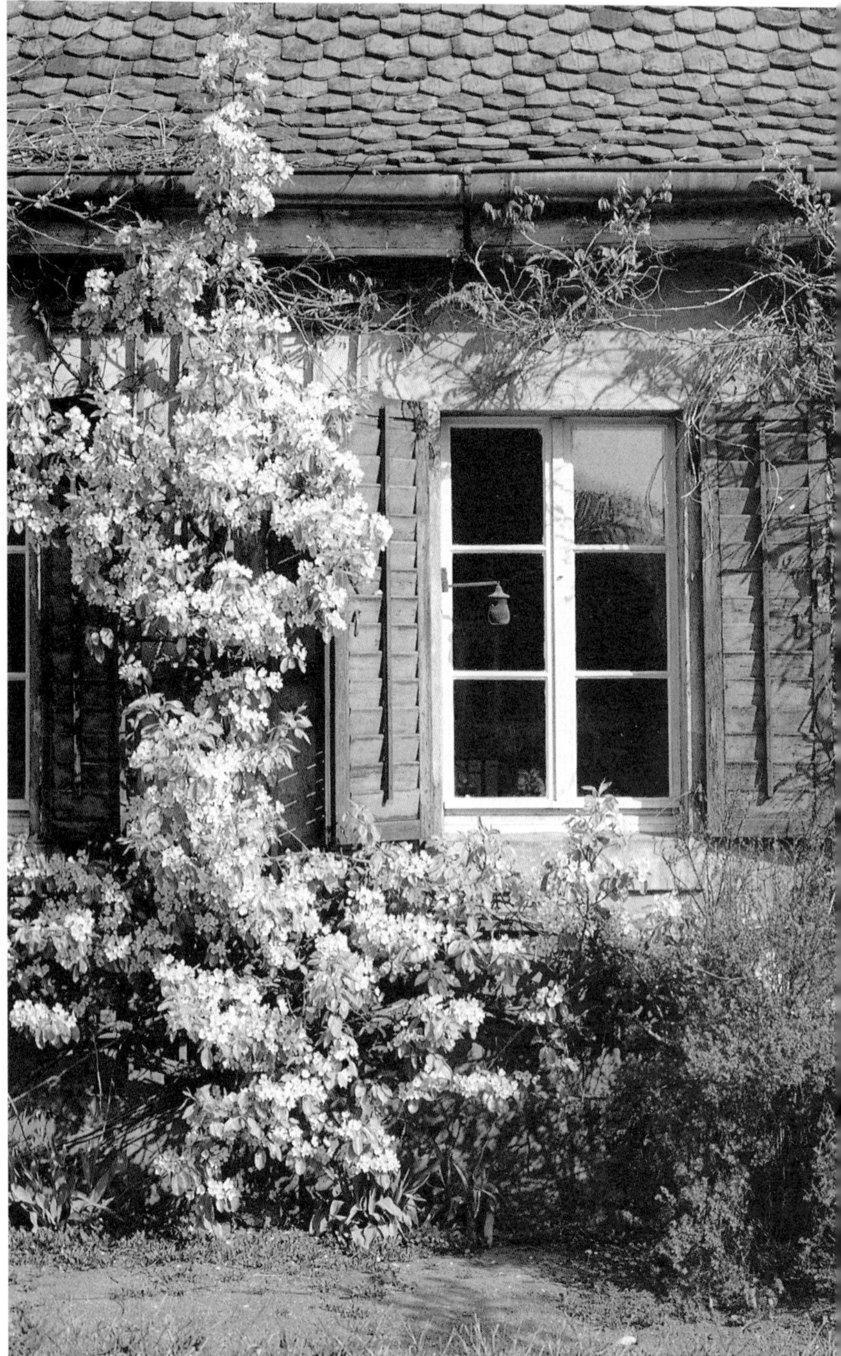

Exposure Modes

Program Auto Exposure Mode

For most snapshot applications you can simply use the mode button to select the P setting (for Programmed exposure control) and let the camera take care of everything. The camera informs you of its choice of shutter speed and aperture inside the viewfinder and on the LCD panel on the back, and a blinking lightning bolt symbol appears to signal that you need to use flash for that particular photo. Although I have found that the basic P mode handles common picture-taking situations very well, the IS cameras offer a variety of other exposure modes for specific subjects or situations and for more advanced photography.

Aperture Priority Mode

In addition to the P mode, the next exposure mode that you should learn to use is the A or Aperture Priority mode. This mode allows you to use the shift buttons in front of the shutter release button on the IS-2 or the Aperture Control button on the IS-10. For the IS-3, use the shift buttons on the back to manually select a lens aperture. Once you have selected the aperture you want, the camera will automatically select the appropriate shutter speed for proper exposure. Why would you want to do this? The answer is depth of field. Depth of field is the amount of the image in front of and behind the plane of focus which also appears to be in sharp focus. This depth of field varies with lens aperture. Larger apertures (smaller f/ numbers) will result in a shallow depth of field, which may be useful when you want to de-emphasize a distracting background or foreground. Conversely, smaller apertures (larger f/ numbers) will increase the depth of field, and may be appropriate for landscapes and other images in which you want both foreground and background in sharp focus. You may find that picking a very small aperture like f/16 or f/22 will result

Using the Program Auto Exposure mode for this tranquil garden shot perfectly rendered both the shadow and highlight detail.

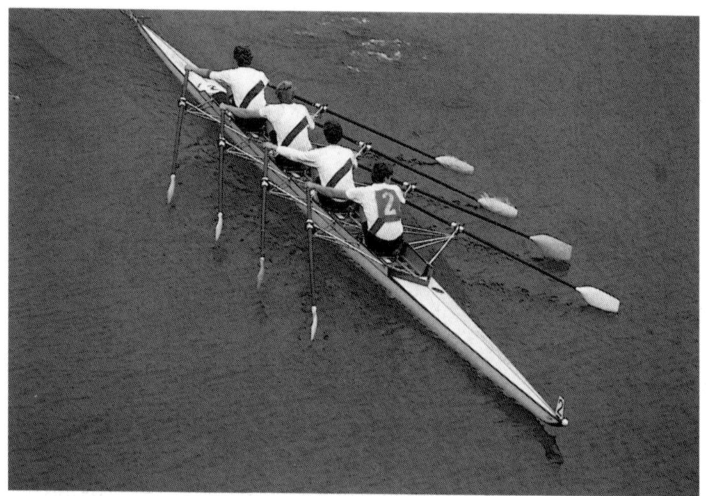

This photo was shot with an IS-3 in S mode. A fast shutter speed of 1/500 was selected in order to freeze the action.

in a shutter speed slower than 1/60 second, in which case you would have to use a tripod to take the picture.

Depth of field always extends 1/3 in front of the plane of focus and 2/3 behind the plane of focus. If you remember this it should help you to visualize the depth of field you will get in your photos.

Shutter Priority Mode

The S or Shutter Priority mode is found only on the IS-3. It allows you to manually select a shutter speed by using the shift collar around the shutter release button. With this mode, the photographer selects a shutter speed from 15 seconds to 1/2,000 second to stop action and the camera picks the appropriate lens aperture for correct exposure. This is particularly useful for fast-moving subjects such as auto races, sports events, children playing and other active subjects.

As illustrated by this photo of two swans, depth of field is the amount of the image in front of and behind the plane of focus (the head of the swan in front) which appears sharp in the picture. ⇨

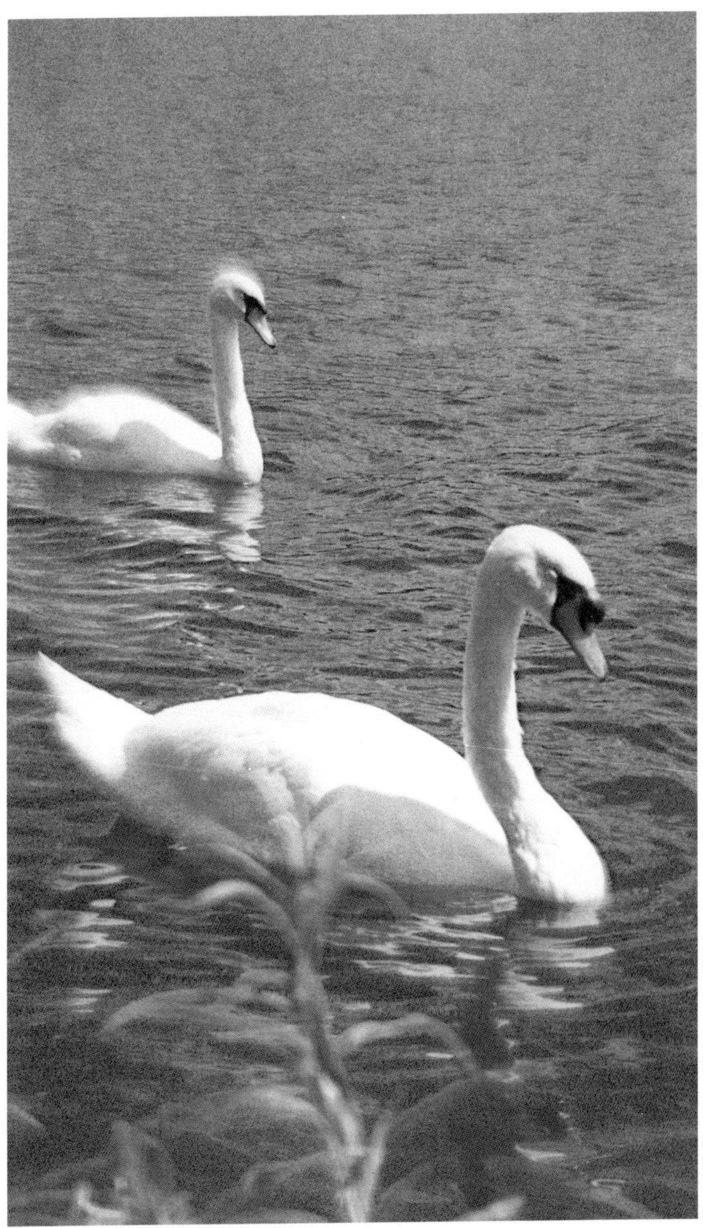

Manual Exposure Mode

Manual exposure mode, available on all the IS cameras except the IS-10, allows you the creative freedom to manually select both shutter speed and lens aperture. On the IS-1 and IS-2, you select the desired lens aperture with the shift buttons in front of the shutter release button. Then you press the shift button on the lower left of the camera back, hold it, and use the same shift buttons in front of the shutter release button to set the desired shutter speed. You will see a + or - displayed in the bottom LCD bar inside the viewfinder and also on the LCD panel on the rear of the camera inside the Mode area. You then adjust shutter speed or aperture or both until both the + and - are visible, which sets the camera for the correct exposure as determined by the camera's built-in meter.

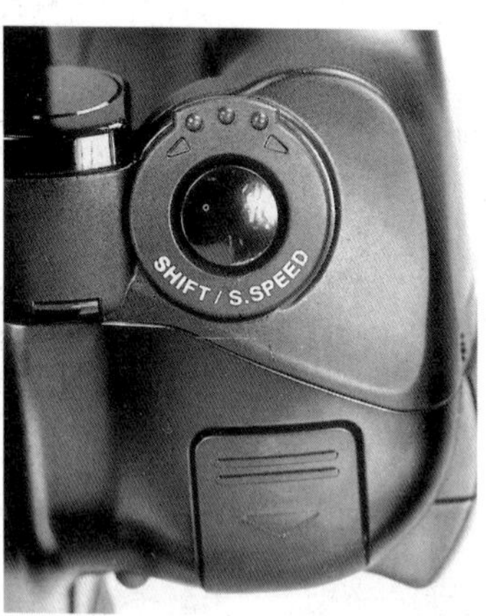

The collar around the shutter release button adjusts the shutter speed.

The procedure is slightly different on the IS-3. On the IS-3 the shutter speeds are set using the collar around the shutter release button. There is a protrusion on the front of this collar which is easily moved by the photographer's right forefinger to select the desired speed. Apertures are then selected with the rocker switch on the right side of the camera back. Correct exposure is indicated by a + and - display inside the viewfinder and on the

The photographer chose a slow shutter speed to blur the running water in this fountain and let the camera select the aperture for correct exposure. A tripod was needed to support the camera because of the slow shutter speed. ⇨

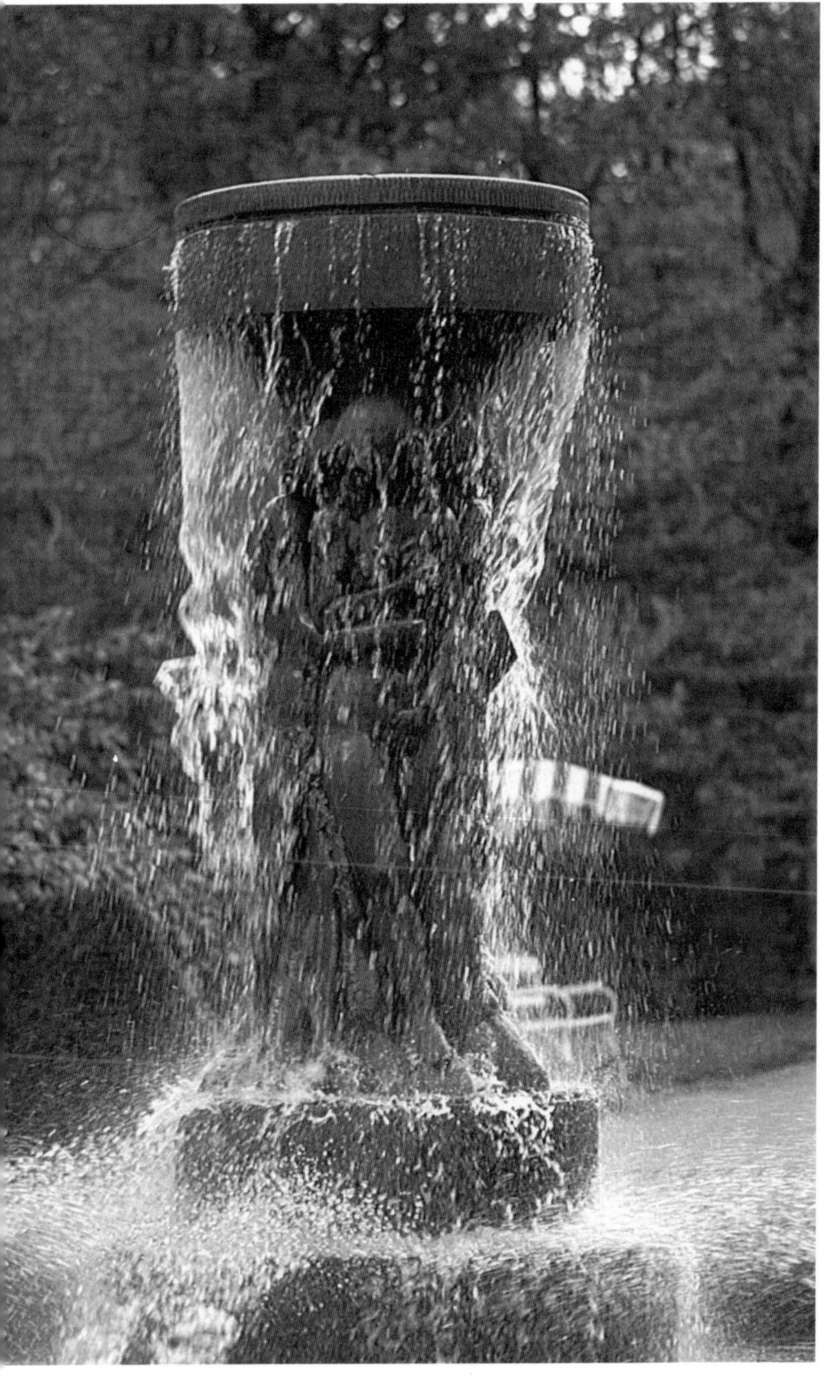

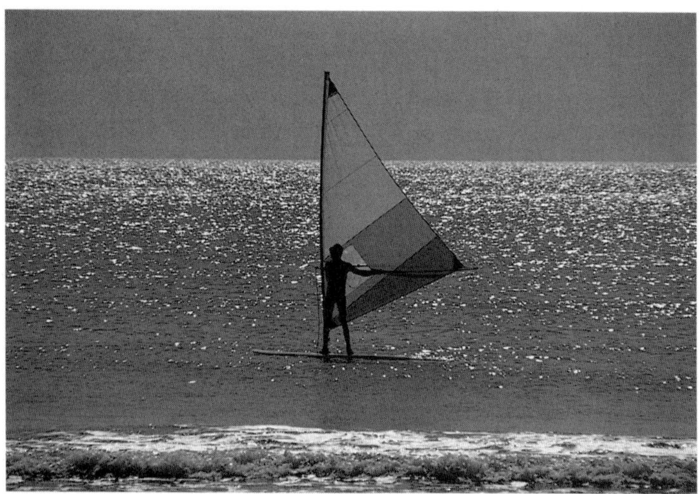

This backlit photo of a windsurfer was taken using M mode. By spot metering on the sail, the photographer captured the person in silhouette. Because of the bright reflections on the water, using the camera's regular, multi-segment meter would have resulted in a very dark picture.

camera back LCD just to the left of the frame counter. Exposure is correct when both + and – are shown. Manual exposure control is most useful in creative picture-taking or in the studio.

Creative use of the Double Exposure mode can create interesting and artistic photographs. The statue was placed in front of a dark background and the first exposure was made with the lens at a wide-angle setting. The lens was then zoomed to 180mm and exposure compensation was set to underexpose the second image slightly. ⇨

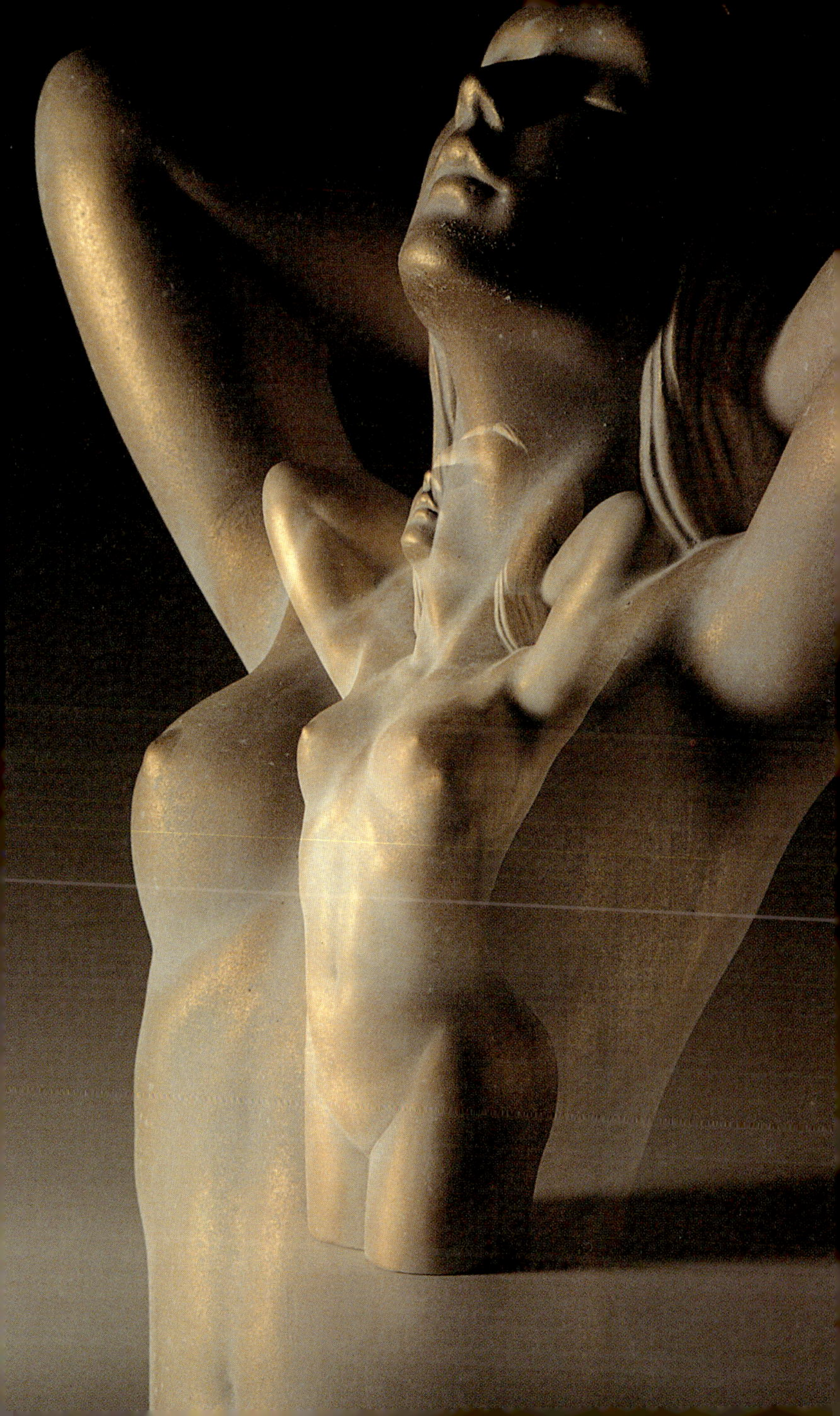

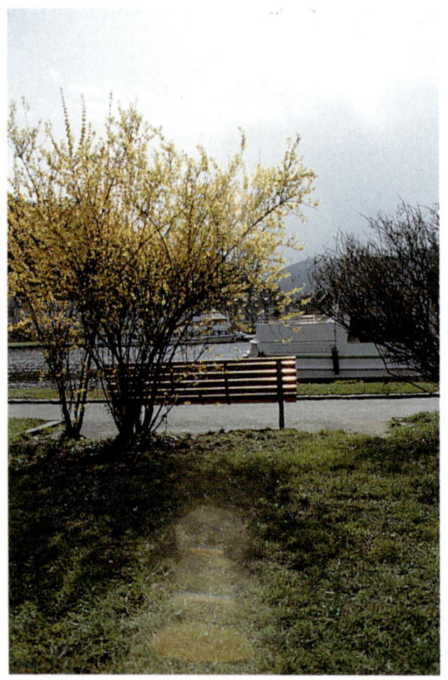

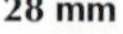

28 mm

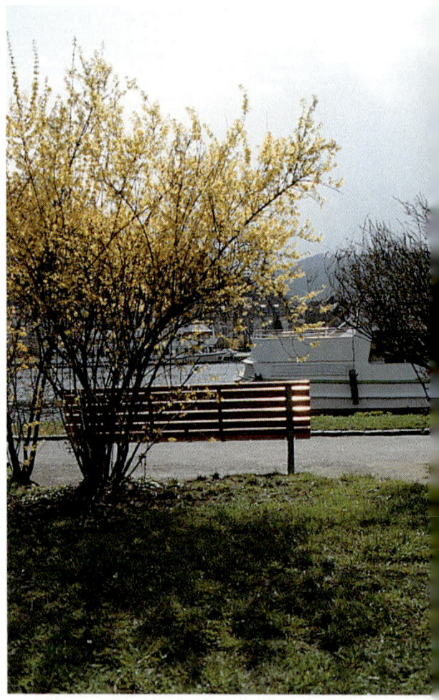

35 mm

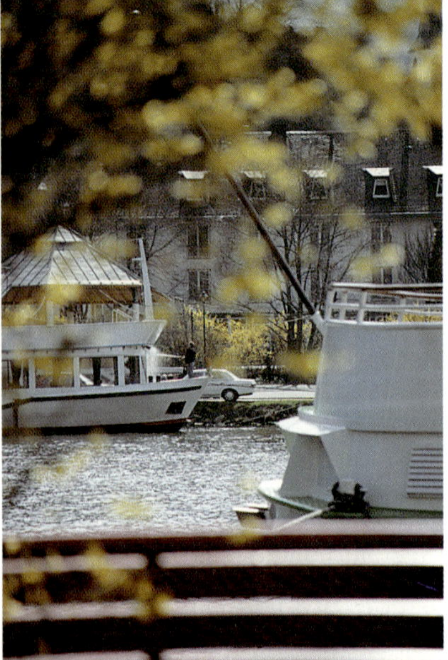

180 mm

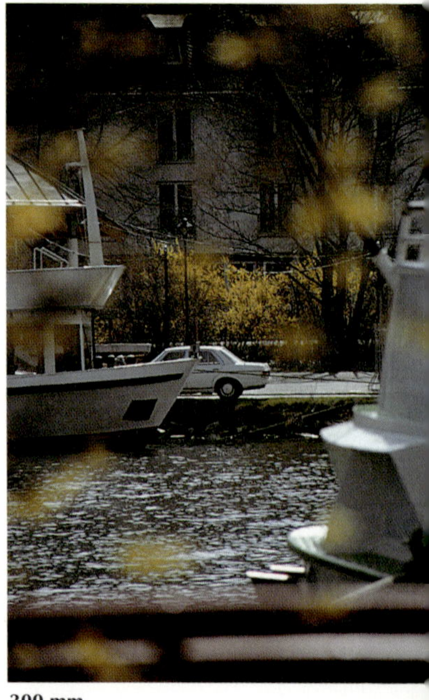

300 mm

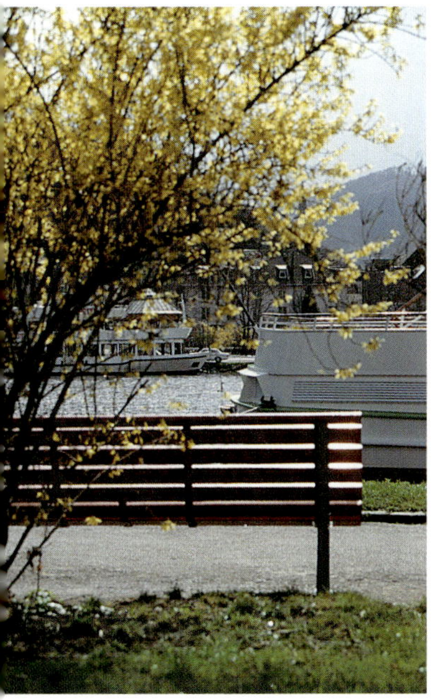

mm

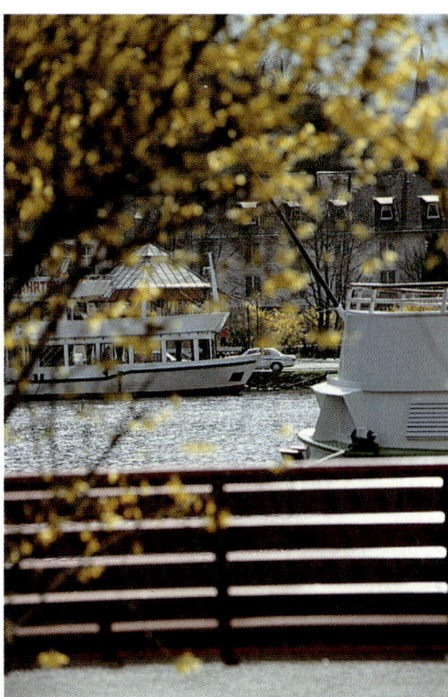

120 mm

The compositional range of a zoom lens is illustrated in this series of photographs. The camera remained in the same position for all six shots while the focal length was adjusted. As the focal length increased, the lens' angle of view decreased causing small details in the 28mm photo to fill the frame at 300mm.

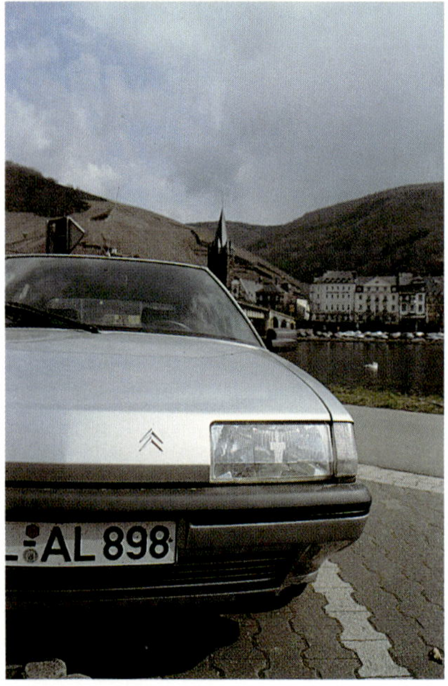

28 mm

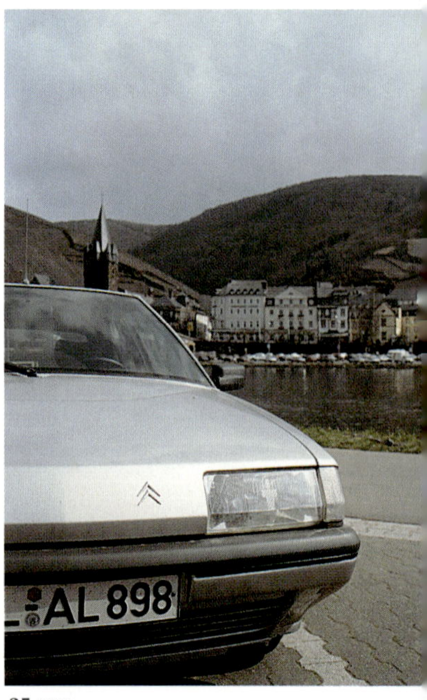

35 mm

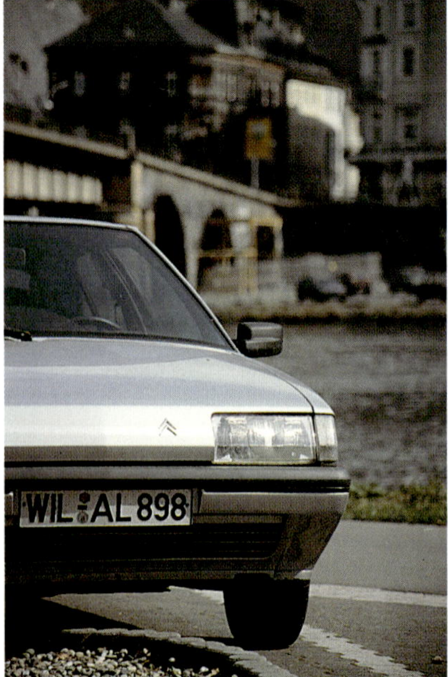

180 mm

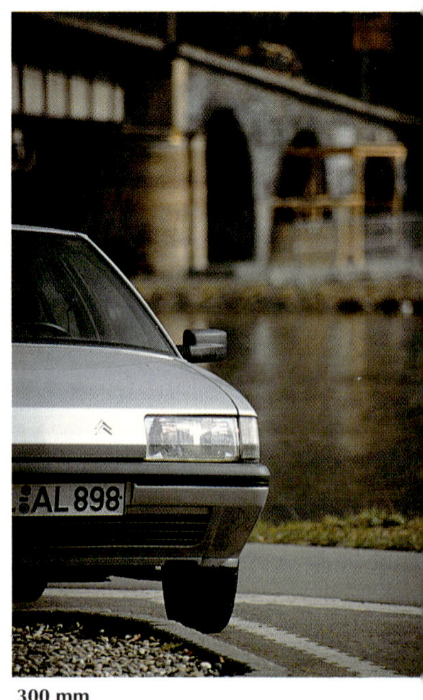

300 mm

mm

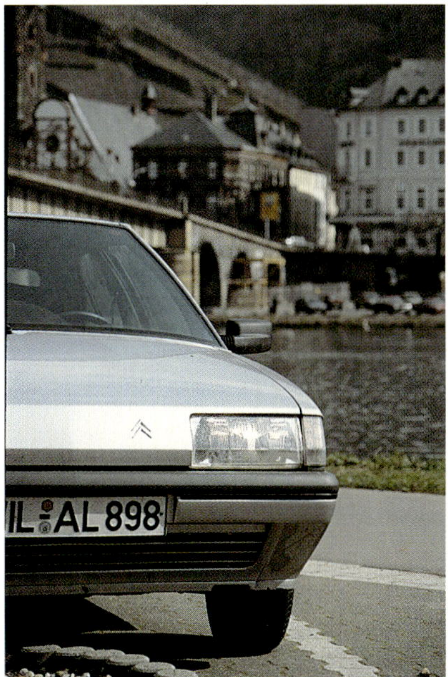

120 mm

The effects of focal length on depth of field and spatial relationships are illustrated in this series of photographs. The camera was repositioned for each shot to keep the car in the foreground approximately the same size. Although the f/stop was not changed, the depth of field decreased dramatically as focal length increased. Also, the angle of view decreased so less of the background can be seen, making the distance between foreground and background appear compressed.

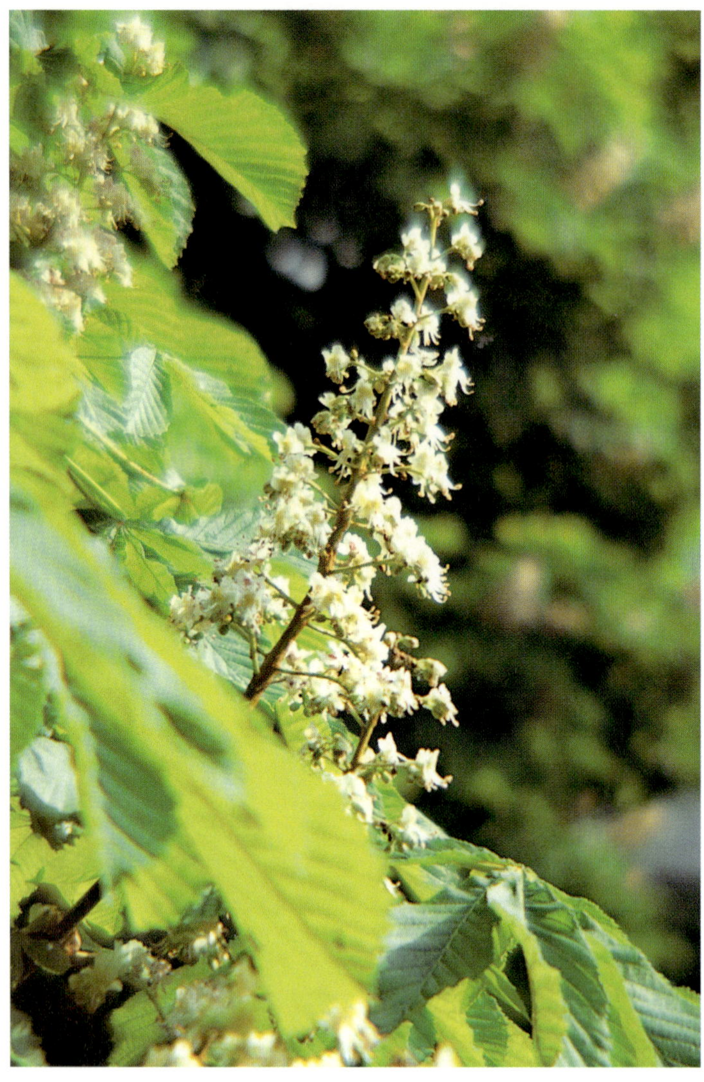

This soft-focus effect was created by using an IS-3 camera with an Olympus Wide-angle Conversion Lens. Instead of using it to convert the camera's 35mm wide-angle setting to 28mm, the lens was set to 180mm. This made it a 144mm lens with less depth of field and soft-focus at the edges.

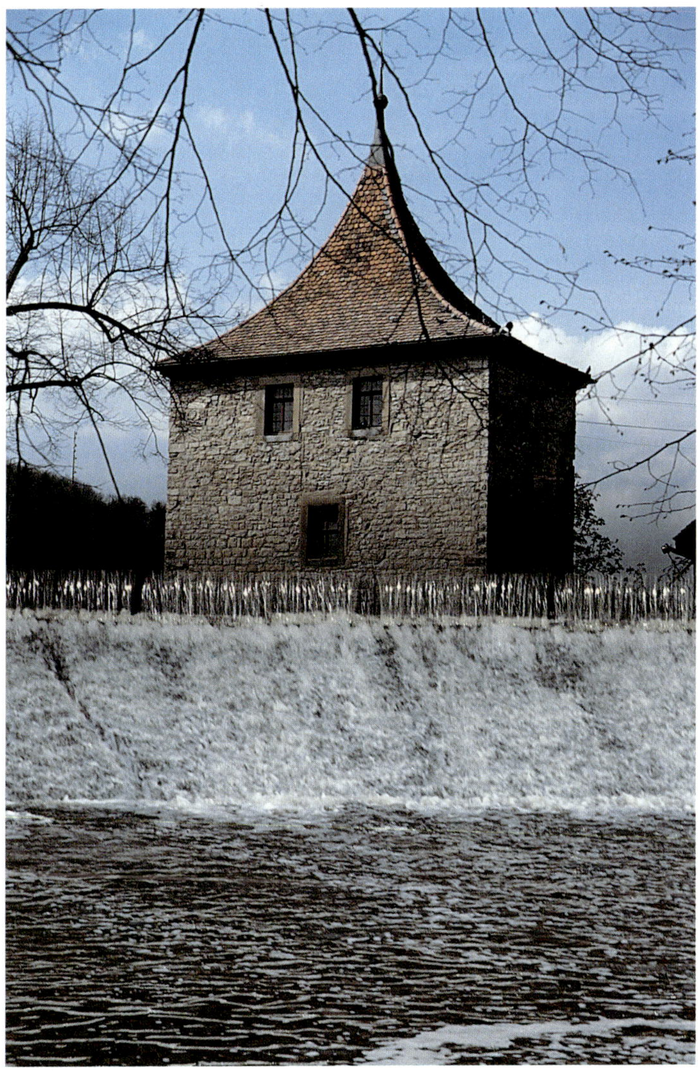

This unusual photograph was created using the camera's Double Exposure mode and a Cokin Double Exposure (or similar) special effects filter. The river was photographed with the filter covering the top half of the film. Then, the filter was turned to cover the bottom half of the film and the building was photographed. Because the portion of film that is covered receives no exposure, compensation is not necesssary.

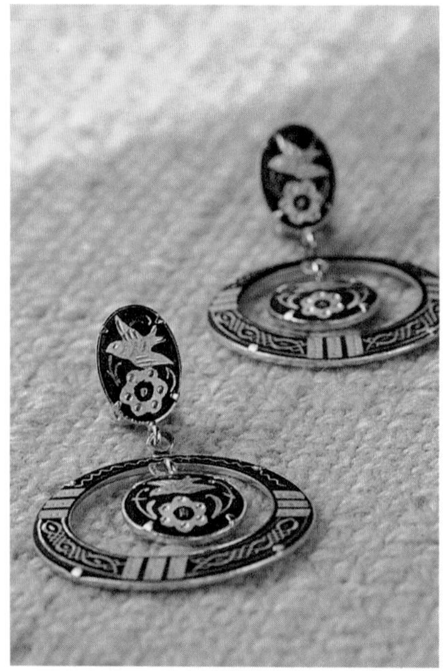

f/22

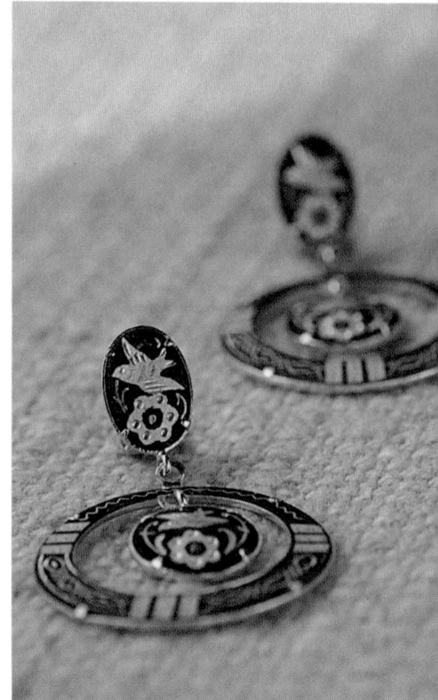

f/11

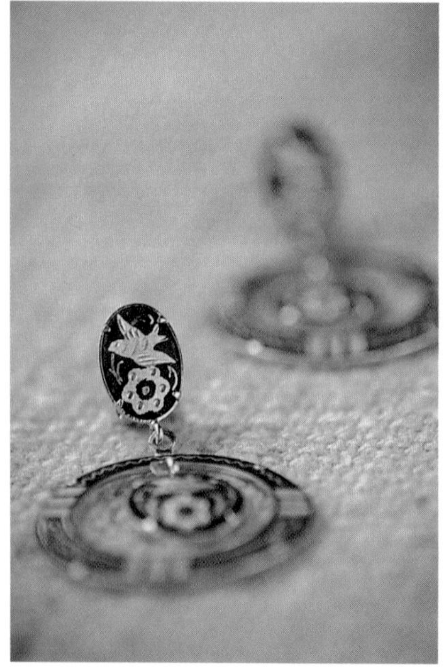

f/5.6

In macro photography, one of the m difficult obstacles to contend with minimal depth of field. With a reprodu tion ratio of 1:3, the top left photo is sh at f/22 which gives approximately 18mm zone of sharpness. At f/11 (t right), the zone narrows to 9mm and f/5.6 (bottom), it is only 5mm wide.

Subject-Specific Programs

The IS cameras also offer several exposure modes which are accessed through pictorial icons on the LCD panel (IS-2 and IS-3) or Mode Selection buttons (IS-10). Night Scene, Portrait and Sports/Action modes are found on the three IS cameras. The IS-3 and IS-10 have added the Landscape mode.

In order to make the best use of the subject-specific programs, the photographer should have a basic knowledge of photographic principles. However, these programs can be used successfully with no prior photographic knowledge. Olympus has developed its own exposure programs for these common applications. With subject-specific programs, even photographers who do not deal with photographic principles on a daily basis can experiment creatively while leaving the technical problem-solving to the camera. These programs are ideal for photographers who want optimal results. Easily recognized icons, or pictograms on the camera's LCD screen facilitate fast selection of the subject-specific programs. After an appropriate setting has been chosen, the photographer need only compose the image and take the picture.

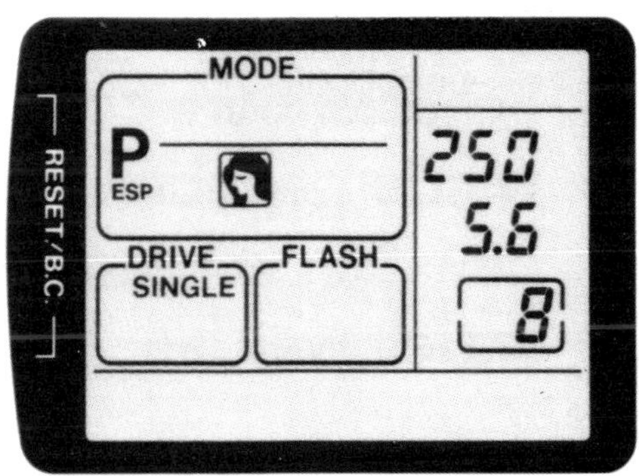

The face icon indicates that the camera is set for the Portrait mode. The shutter speed is 1/250 and the aperture is f/5.6 as seen on the right side of the IS-3's LCD panel.

Portrait Program

This program was adapted to two typical types of pictures, the head-and-shoulders shot and the full portrait. The aperture will open to its largest setting, f/5.6 at the telephoto setting and f/4.5 at the wide angle setting. Very fast shutter speeds will result in an incremental closing of the aperture.

The advantage to having the camera choose a wide aperture lies in selective focus, which dissolves even a highly distracting or annoying background to a pleasant blur. This is usually desired in most portrait photographs to ensure the person is the point of interest. To maximize this effect, there should be a substantial amount of separation between the subject and background. Objects behind the subject become less and less sharp as their distance from the subject increases.

Although the Portrait program will work on any focal length setting, using a telephoto setting (longer than 50mm) is recommended. This crops in tighter on the person or people and eliminates unwanted elements in the photograph. Also, longer focal lengths produce a more pleasing perspective for portraiture. Most people have seen the distortion caused by a wide angle lens; a telephoto lens has the opposite effect. As a lens' focal length increases and the f/stop remains constant, the depth of field decreases.

When the subject's head and shoulders fill the frame in the viewfinder, the autofocus frame should be directed at the subject's eyes, the release button pressed lightly, and then pressed the rest of the way only when the subject has been framed as desired. This procedure must be followed, otherwise the person's neck will be in perfect focus but the eyes will not. After each shot the focusing field must be positioned again on the eyes and the setting locked in with gentle pressure on the shutter release button.

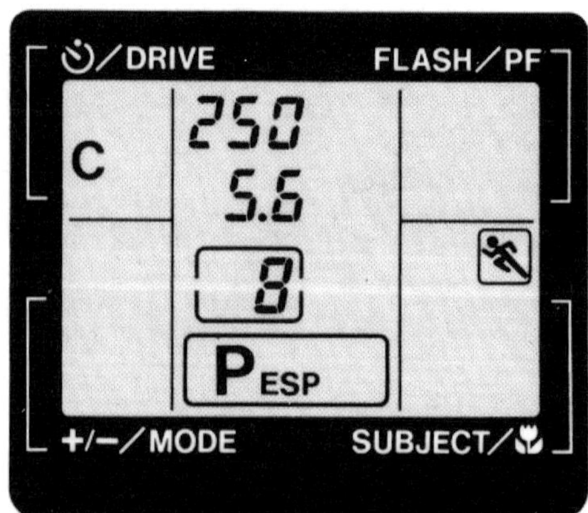

The runner icon, shown here on the LCD of the IS-2, denotes the Sport/ Action program mode. The shutter speed is 1/250 and the drive is set for continuous film advance.

Sports/Action Program

The Sports/Action program is the ideal automatic mode when pictures are blurred despite all the fully automatic features. This program produces super sharp pictures of all normal fast-moving tourist or family events. Therefore, it is the ideal program for snapshots! Of course, it is also possible to obtain sharp sports photographs using the sports program. The emphasis is on "it is possible!" Anyone going to a Formula-1 race without first trying out the sports program should not be surprised if success is limited. It is just not possible to pull out a camera at the last moment, press the release and obtain a complete roll of spectacularly focused pictures. It takes experience to predict the exciting moments of the sport being photographed, but the program can reduce the technical aspects of shooting to simply pressing the shutter release.

Movements are to be frozen and reproduced in sharp focus. This is not accomplished with the largest lens aperture; the high shutter speed has priority. If there is more light, first and foremost the shutter speed is increased. Up to a maximum of three speeds are available. The aperture will close as the speed is increased

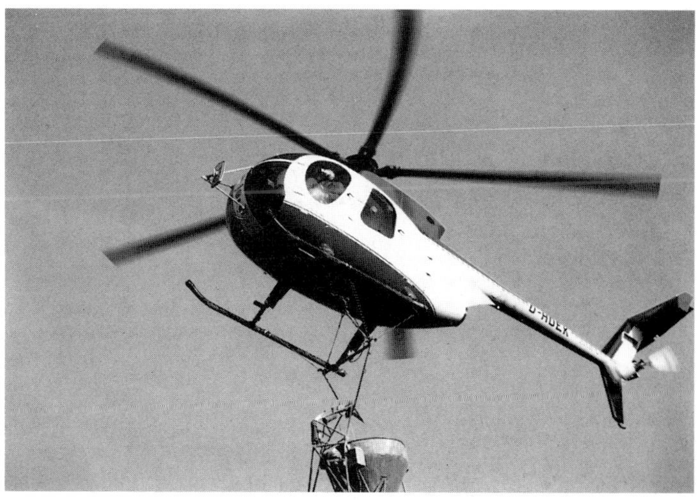

By using the Sports/Action mode, the photographer was able to capture the helicopter frozen in mid-air.

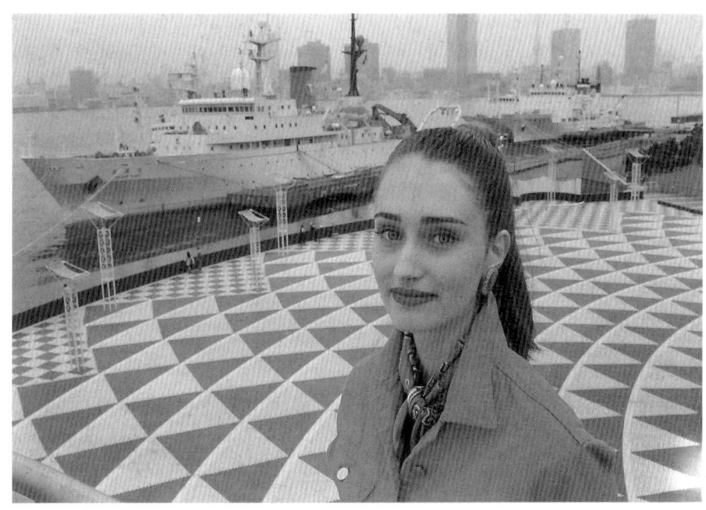

The Landscape program sets exposure favoring a small aperture for greater depth of field. It is the ideal program if you want to photograph a person and show their surroundings.

only when the maximum value has been reached due to sufficient illumination of the subject. The programmed control system automatically adjusts the drive mode to continuous film advance for this subject-specific program.

Landscape Program

Despite the program's name, it shouldn't be reserved for photographing landscapes only. The concept of landscape refers to a subject-specific program which controls exposure with a bias towards the smallest possible aperture for greater depth of field. This makes it the ideal program for those vacation photos with your family standing in front of a monument or scenic view. You can focus on people in the foreground, and be assured that the spectacular background will also be clear.

The photographer needs to keep an eye on the shutter speed, especially with low film speeds. Shutter speeds may become too slow for handholding. After all, taking pictures of landscapes is rarely a fast-paced endeavor. For the same reason, single frame advance is designated by the camera when set on the landscape symbol.

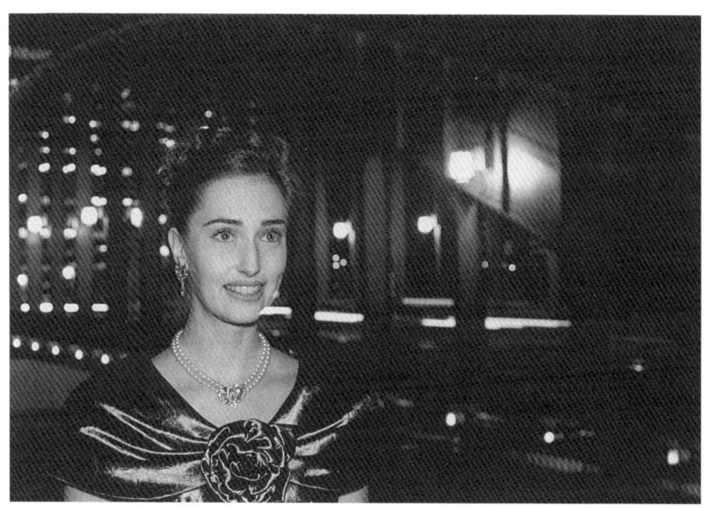

The bottom photo was taken using only flash to expose the subject. In the top photo, using flash with the Night Scene program exposed the subject properly and kept the shutter open to expose the background with ambient light.

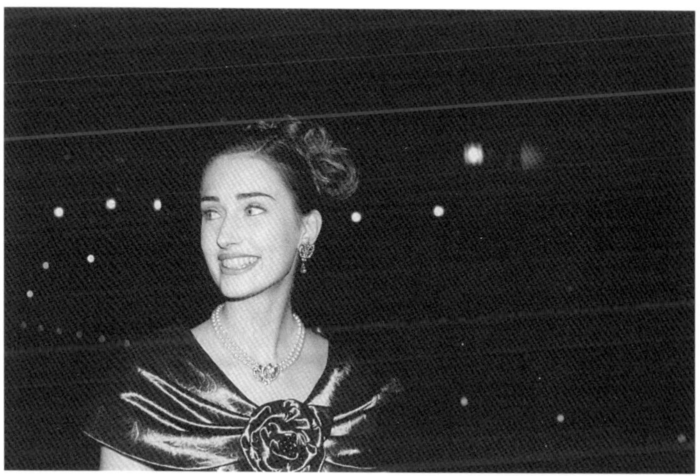

An analysis of many thousands of landscape pictures has shown that nature scenes are usually located in the infinity or close-to-infinity distance range. When there is depth in an image, it should be in focus from front to back in the picture. Therefore, this program provides a small aperture opening for an extended depth of field range. Setting the camera's zoom lens to a short focal length of 28 to 35mm is highly suitable and recommended in Landscape Program mode for panoramic views.

Night Scene Program

Basically, the Night Scene program automatically balances the existing light exposure on the background with flash exposure on the main subject for photographs with ambience. Anytime a scene has a beautiful or interesting ambient light that you would like to capture in a photograph, such as a sunset, a cityscape, neon lights, or a lit Christmas tree, this is the mode to use. The flash will properly expose subjects in the foreground without any complicated calculations on the part of the photographer. If there is no foreground subject, this mode can also be used without flash for exposures up to fifteen seconds long.

In this mode, the camera's micro computer measures the brightness of the background and determines the aperture and shutter speed. The amount of flash required is based on the distance to the main subject and the predetermined aperture value. The shutter can remain open for as long as several seconds to expose the background, so a tripod is recommended.

Macro Mode

All IS cameras, except the IS-10, also feature a "macro" mode for very close focus. This is accessed by selecting the icon of a flower on the IS-2's LCD panel or by pushing the button on the lens barrel of the IS-3. The IS-1 allows an additional "wide macro" setting, which switches the lens to 40mm and sets it for close focus. The IS-2 lacks this, but offers a "super macro" mode which allows you to focus only 1.3 feet (0.39 m) from the subject so that a subject area of 4-3/4 X 7-1/16 inches (12 X 18 cm) fills the frame. With the optional A-Macro H.Q. Converter, the IS-2 can get down to life size on the film. The IS-3 offers macro focus down to about 1 foot (.3 m) from the subject. Although the IS-10 does not have a separate macro mode, the camera can focus down to 2.5 feet (.75 m).

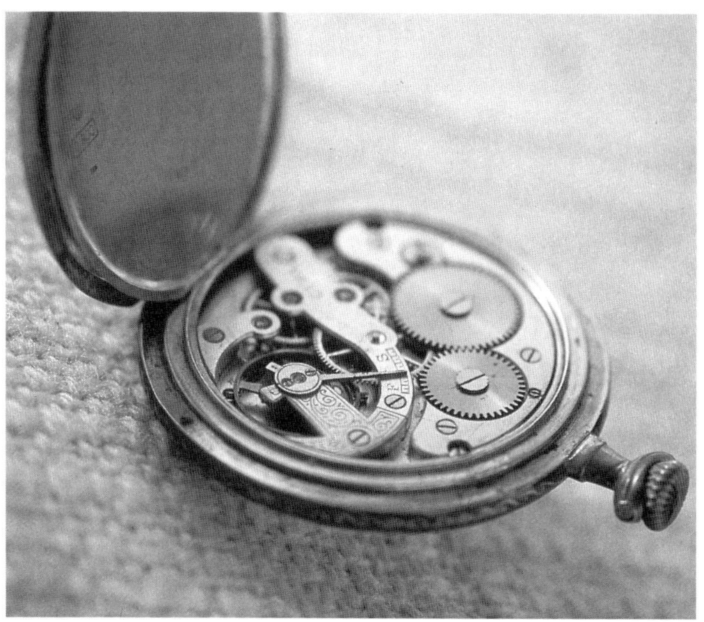

In Macro mode, the IS cameras can focus quite close on an object. Using as small an aperture as possible is recommended for close-up photography, as the depth of field is very narrow.

Exposure Compensation

Most films respond best when exposed at the manufacturer's film speed rating but there are times when you may want to alter this for special purposes. The Olympus IS cameras, except the IS-10, have an exposure compensation control which allows you to adjust the film speed selected by the camera. By the use of this control, you can increase or decrease the speed of the film in 1/3 stop increments up to +/- 4 full stops.

The DX coding system on the IS 1 and IS-2 cameras can set only film speeds of 25, 32, 50, 100, 200, 400, 800, 1600 and 3200. If you load a film with a speed in between these, the camera will automatically be set for the next lower setting. For example, if you load some ISO 64 Ektachrome film, the camera will automatically be set for ISO 50, but you can use the exposure compensation control to boost the speed by 1/3 stop to get an accurate 64 speed. Either plan to only use films which fall on the available DX code film speeds, or set the exposure compensation control accordingly. Because the number of film speed settings has been increased, this is unlikely to be a problem with the IS-3 and IS-10 cameras.

When Auto Exposure Does Not Work

It is very important to realize that there are situations in which the camera's built-in meter will not give correct exposure information. This is not a problem specific to Olympus IS cameras, but applies equally to any camera's metering system. This section offers a brief summation of the situations in which even the highly accurate IS meters may not give correct exposure information and some practical suggestions on how to get good exposures under difficult conditions.

To understand why the camera's meter does not always give the best exposure information, you must understand how an SLR camera's built-in meter measures light. Light meters are designed on the assumption that subjects will have an equal amount of light and dark areas, which is usually true. Therefore, meters will choose an exposure setting to render the scene as middle gray, also called 18% gray.

Simply stated, the auto exposure system of an Olympus IS camera will give incorrect exposure information whenever the overall reflectance of the scene is much greater or much less than 18%. The important point to remember is that the camera will determine an exposure which will render the scene as though its reflectance is 18%. Very bright subjects will be too dark, very dark subjects will be too light.

I have previously explained that you may use the Exposure Compensation control on your camera to program the camera with a factor of over- or underexposure. When photographing very bright or light colored subjects this would require a plus factor - that is an overexposure factor - because this will offset the camera's tendency to underexpose light subjects and render them too dark. In the opposite situation - dark subjects which reflect little light - the required factor would be an underexposure or minus value to offset the camera's tendency to overexpose such subjects.

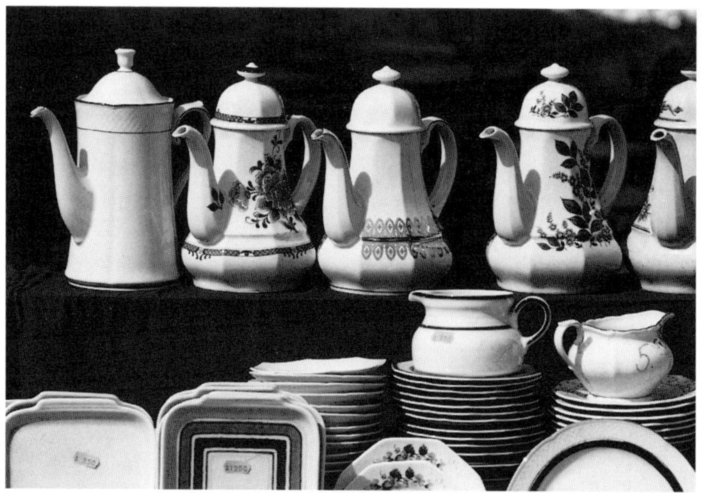

This interesting arrangement of teapots and china was spotted at a flea market. The camera was set to Program mode and exposure compensation was set to overexpose the image slightly so the porcelain photographed as white.

Unusual Exposure Situations

When you are shooting rapidly and encounter a subject of high or low reflectance and only expect to take a few photos of that subject, you may not want to set the Exposure Compensation control. Instead, you may prefer to use an alternate metering method. Seek a subject which is under the same light as the subject you wish to photograph, but has a closer to average reflectance. You would then take a light meter reading from that subject and photograph your intended subject at the same exposure. This is easiest to do in the Manual mode. Although you can hold a set of exposure values by lightly pressing on the shutter release button, this also locks and holds the focus, and it is rare that your alternate subject will have the required reflectance and be at the same distance as your main subject. Of course, if you wish to maintain automatic exposure you may switch the camera to manual focus. Which works best will depend on the specific situation.

Another method for coping with this sort of photographic situation is to find a small area of the subject which has more normal reflectance and take a spot meter reading from that area. This works well as long as the area is no smaller than the spot metering circle in the camera viewfinder. Pressing in on the spot metering button with your right thumb takes the reading and holds it as long as you keep the button depressed. It does not activate the autofocus mechanism, which you operate in the normal manner by light pressure on the shutter release button. In this way you may take a spot meter reading of the best area of the subject and then hold that reading while recomposing and focusing the image. I have found this to be the fastest method for metering under many different situations. It is particularly good for backlit situations.

Fireworks: There are some specific situations in which taking a meter reading of any sort is impossible. A common example is a fireworks display. Even the Olympus IS camera's spotmeter is no help here! Since your reaction time is not fast enough to fire the shutter at the proper point, this type of photography is best done with the camera mounted on a good tripod. The shutter should be set to "blb" (stands for "bulb" and means the shutter stays open as long as you maintain pressure on the shutter release button) and opened prior to the firing of the rocket. You may leave the shutter open for several rockets if the sky is very dark; otherwise, you should only get one or two on a frame. With the shutter set to "blb" suggested f/ stops for fireworks are: f/16 for 400 speed film, f/11 for 200, f/8 for 100. Using film faster than 400 is not recommended as it will be too likely to pick up overall exposure from ambient light and render the background gray instead of black. Since the camera will have difficulty finding focus during an actual fireworks display, it may be necessary to use manual, "power" focus with the IS-2 or IS-3. Another solution is to prefocus on a different subject of equal distance (probably infinity) and then be ready to fire when the rocket is launched.

Thunderstorms: Thunderstorms are another opportunity for really unusual photos; just remember that they are dangerous. If you want to take photos of lightning, be sure that you are at a safe dis-

As the main subject of this photograph, the exposure of the clown, could have been improved slightly by taking a manual reading on the subject. The photographer could also have applied the "Sunny 16 Rule" which would have resulted in less exposure of the highlights. ⇨

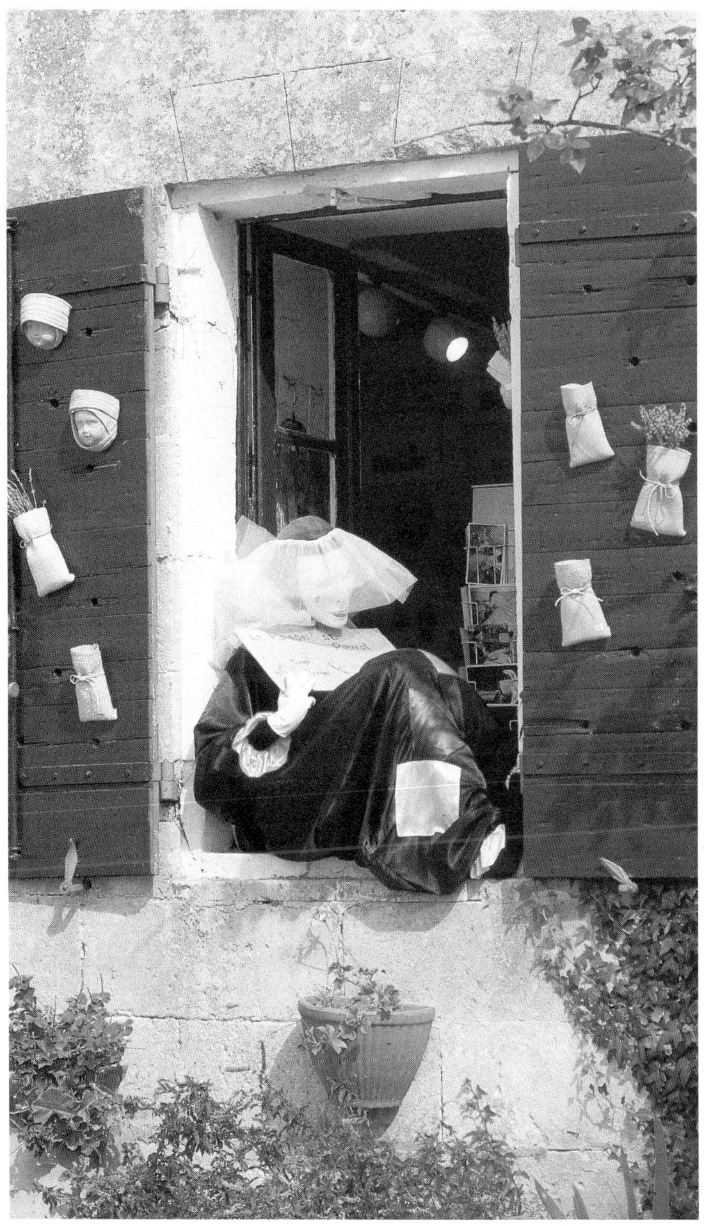

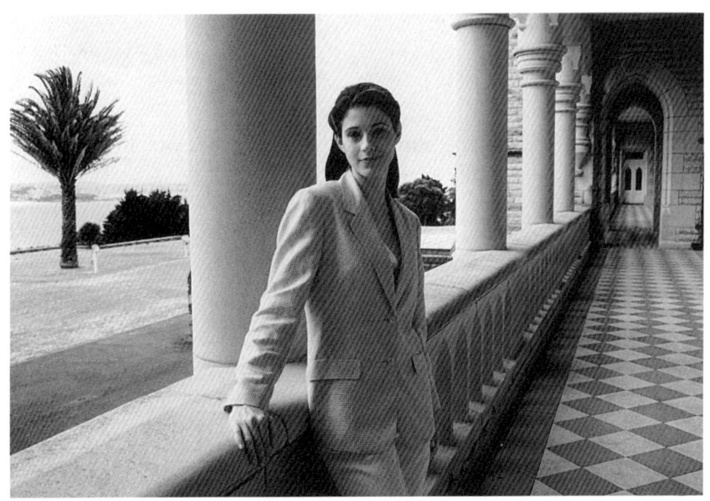

Although the Olympus metering system is extremely accurate, difficult lighting situations can fool the camera's meter. In the bottom photo, the bright background biased the exposure reading, causing the subject to be underexposed. Using the camera's spot metering feature to take a light reading off the woman's face produced an accurate exposure.

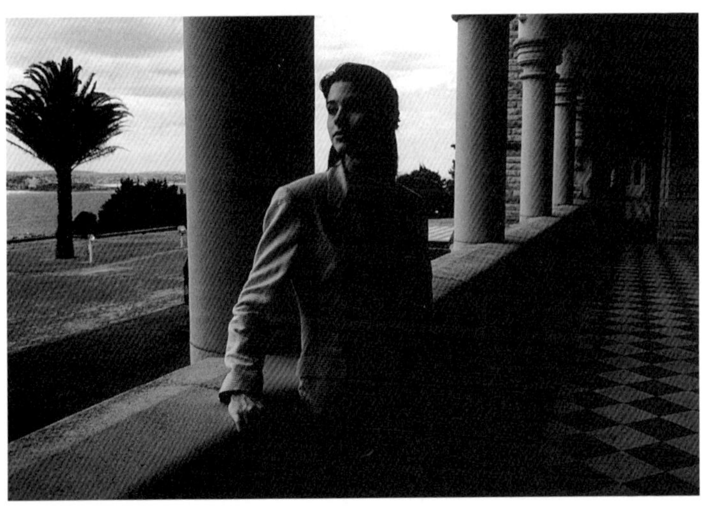

tance from the storm itself. Never allow yourself to be the tallest object around during a thunderstorm. You will be acting just like a lightning rod! For thunderstorms at night, the above recommended exposures for fireworks will be a good starting point. Daytime thunderstorm photos are almost impossible because the ambient light level is usually too high to allow the long exposures which would be needed to capture several lightning bolts.

Concerts: Another difficult exposure situation is photographing stage shows or concerts. If you just use the standard auto exposure modes, you will get photos in which too much of the dark background has influenced the exposure and the stage will be too light. You should try to get in close enough to take a Manual mode light reading with the spot meter of just one of the performers and use this exposure for all of your photos. Remember that the exposure determined up close will be correct no matter how far you get from the stage. For heaven's sake, don't make yourself look ridiculous by firing off your flash from the back rows of a concert. It will have no effect at all at those distances.

If you are unable to get close enough to take a good meter reading, here are some suggested settings which work well for me. If you are dealing with spotlighted performers, as is usually the case at concerts, the best exposure with 400 speed film will be about 1/250 at f/2.8. If you are photographing stage shows, plays and the like which are usually lighted with floods, exposure will be about 1/125 at f/2.8. Although the color temperature of stage lighting is not really matched for daylight type color film, I have found that my best results were made with this type of film, particularly when colored spotlights are used.

Copy Work: Photographing flat artwork requires precise alignment of the original and the camera. The film plane and the original need to be parallel, or the resulting photographic copy will not be in proportion. In addition, uniform illumination across the surface of the original is required. Flash is generally not recommended, because there is no way to preview the lighting. Photo floodlights or even diffused sunlight may be used as long as the subject is lighted evenly. A polarizing filter will reduce unwanted reflections and is a necessity if the original has a glossy finish or is under glass. Low-sensitivity, fine-grained films (ISO 25 to ISO 50)

A typical copystand set-up consists of a column mounted on a baseboard and may or may not include lighting. The camera attaches to an adjustable mount with a 1/4"-20 screw which fits the camera's tripod mounting socket.

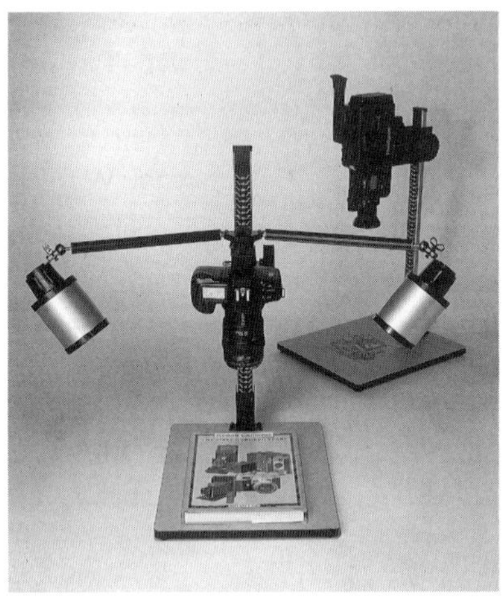

should be used for clarity and sharpness. A tripod or copy stand is needed for steady camera support at slow shutter speeds and to keep the camera level.

Automatic metering only produces a correct exposure when the metered zone of the original is approximately 18% reflective. Using a gray card would be a more accurate way to determine the exposure values. However, there is no way to lock in the exposure reading from a gray card. Either use manual mode to set exposure or take a meter reading from the gray card and the original, and set exposure compensation for the difference between the two.

Festivals: Subjects at carnivals, fairs and ethnic festivals are best captured with the Sports/Action program. If it is a sunny day, use fill flash for snapshots of people and other close subjects, especially if they are backlighted. For photographing the event at night, try the Night Scene program with flash. In the Sports/Action program, the flash constitutes the main light and the background of the picture will remain dark. In the Night Scene program, flash will illuminate elements in the foreground, such as a person, and the shutter will remain open to allow the background to be lighted by ambient light. This really captures the festive mode in your pictures if there is a colorfully-lighted midway or carnival rides behind the subject. Properly exposed photos of the festival lights can also be created using Night Scene program without flash. For an interesting effect, photograph a lighted Ferris wheel or other ride with a slow shutter speed while it is moving. Don't forget to use a tripod.

Flowers: Try to compose photographs of flowers so they stand out against a plain background. With flash, use a small aperture to limit the flash range and prevent the background from being illuminated. A small card, approximately one foot square, with white on one side and black on the other can act as a reflector or a background. Get out early to photograph flowers with the morning dew still on them or go out shooting after a gentle rain. The water droplets add sparkling highlights and a feeling of freshness. If you're not an early riser, bring a spray bottle along and lightly mist flowers and foliage for the same effect.

Macro mode allows you to focus the lens with the camera closer to the subject. The IS-2 camera offers a Super Macro mode, allowing the camera to be focused as close as 1.5 feet at a fixed 70mm focal length. The camera's zoom lens can focus at 2 feet from 35 to 100mm. The IS-3's Macro mode allows for photographs as close as 2 feet from 35 to 120mm. Although the IS-10 does not offer a macro mode, the lens can be focused as close as 2.5 feet from the subject at any focal length. In addition, adding close-up filters or an Olympus macro converter lens will allow the subject to be reproduced even larger on the film. Remember, if there are leaves, stems or branches near the center of the viewfinder, they will interfere with the autofocus system; in this case, manual focus is the best solution.

Parties and occasions: To avoid photographer stress, set the camera on the Program mode and leave the rest to automatic control. The camera ensures optimal exposure balance of flash and ambient light in bright rooms. If mood and atmosphere are to be dominant, special effects may be achieved with flash and time exposures in Aperture Priority mode.

Use a wide-angle setting for a group shot of everyone and a telephoto setting to snap candid pictures of people from a distance as they enjoy themselves. When wide-angle direct-flash shots are taken, only the adjusted shooting distance is illuminated optimally. The loss of illumination on the background is significant. If available, an accessory flash unit should be used for bounce flash exposures. Bounce flash and a long flash-to-subject shooting dis-

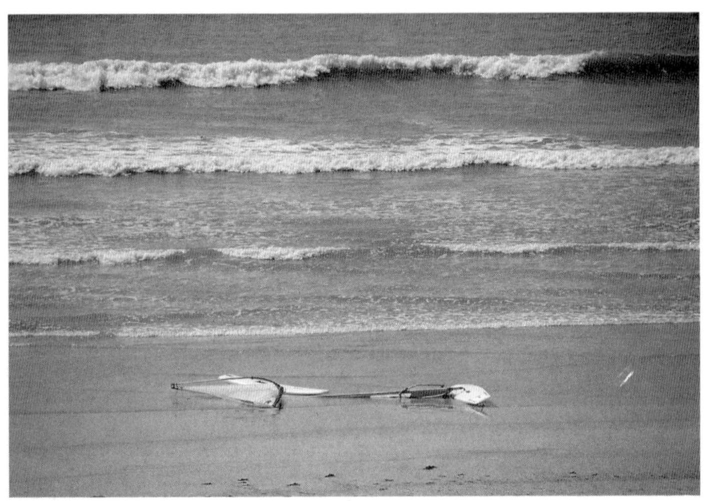

A fast shutter speed was used to freeze these ocean waves as they rolled in.

tance should be used for subjects covering extended depth ranges such as people at a dining-room table. Also, for portraits or small groups where people are looking directly at the camera, don't forget to use the Auto S flash mode for red-eye reduction.

Water: This relatively difficult subject often requires long exposure times because motion blurs accentuating the water's flow can be desirable when taking pictures of brooks, rapids or waterfalls. This requires a tripod and a series of shots beginning with the smallest aperture and aperture priority (Av) to test the effect.

On calm days lakes, ponds and canals frequently provide brilliant reflections which produce the most intense colors with the sun at the photographer's back using a polarizing filter to intensify the effect. A wide-angle lens setting allows for photographing closer to the water, using the Landscape program.

Weddings: Follow the same general guidelines as "Parties and Occasions". In addition to the Program mode, the Portrait program can be effective for trouble-free, well-exposed pictures. It is also a good exposure mode choice because it automatically uses

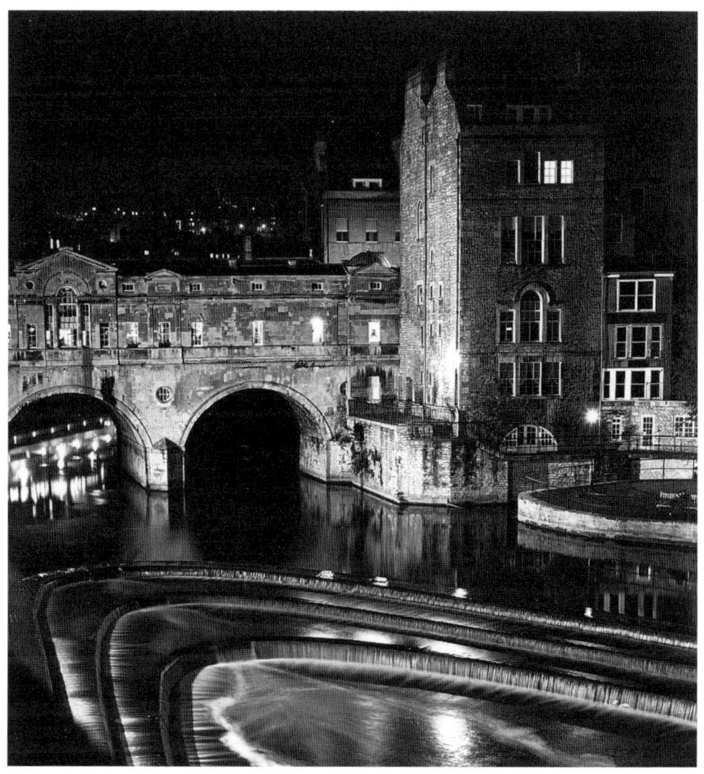

When you are traveling, don't leave your camera in the hotel room after the sun goes down. This long exposure of Bath, England at night captures the city in a different light. Photo: Paul Comon

as large an aperture as possible. Smaller apertures restrict the shooting range of the flash too much. Backlighting is almost always a problem at weddings. Keep the flash set for fill for photographs taken outside in bright sun and shade or in rooms with light coming in through windows. To capture the bride coming down the isle, focus in advance on a spot on the floor or the edge of a pew at a point that will make a good shot. Then recompose and wait till the bride reaches the spot and shoot. Remember that the subject must not be farther away than the range of the flash.

Snow scenes: Grazing light gives snow-covered fields more depth. Backlighting is the most effective but also most difficult type of lighting. At high altitudes, a polarizing filter will produce an almost black sky. Therefore, a skylight filter should be used to prevent excessive blue coloration in the shadow areas. Spot metering on a substitute 18% gray surface or Kodak Gray Card is recommended.

Photographs taken of falling snow require extremely slow shutter speeds. A large foreground and a relatively dark background are desirable. Exposures of snow-covered fields taken at dusk or night are particularly effective. With Aperture Priority mode, they are easy to photograph or take a series of exposures with minus corrections only.

10 Tips for Better Travel Pictures

1. Make plans and check equipment, especially batteries, in advance.
2. Try to shoot evocative rather than just illustrative pictures. Do not confine yourself to strict documentation. Try to capture moods.
3. Learn to observe. Often patience is more important than any staging.
4. Move as close as possible to the subject.
5. Instead of capturing an extensive exposure series using the same framing, really examine the subject by taking shots from different perspectives.
6. Do not just change the focal length. Change the distance and hence the perspective. Try to take photographs from the perspective of a frog or bird.
7. Force yourself to see image compositions and graphic relationships consciously. Only those who master the rules of classic image composition will be able to break them.
8. Always aspire for the best optical and technical quality in your pictures. To achieve this, examine the viewfinder image carefully. Use a tripod or monopod, polarization filters and fill flash.
9. Take pictures in extreme lighting and weather situations and at unconventional times of the day such as early in the morning or at dusk.
10. Always ask permission before taking pictures of people.

Creative Lighting Control

Although much of the previous text of this book has been devoted to the many ways in which the Olympus IS cameras have made it possible to determine perfect exposure, there may be times when the best exposure from a technical point of view is not the one you want. You may want to convey a special feeling which the normal exposure simply does not do. There are many types of photographs in which this situation may come up, but the two which will be encountered most often are called high-key and low-key photographs.

In a high-key photograph, the tonal range has been entirely shifted toward highlight. There are no blacks and little in the way of dark areas. The photo is technically overexposed, but this has been done intentionally to produce a light, soft effect. Colors tend to be rendered in pastel shades. Bridal shots and portraits of children are two of the most typical subjects for high-key lighting. To successfully create high-key photographs, you must be able to control your lighting, or work in a situation which produces the lighting best suited to this effect. This is soft lighting without much contrast, typical of a hazy overcast day outdoors in which shadows are indistinct. In the studio, such lighting is usually produced by large soft boxes, such as the Multidome made by Photoflex.

This soft lighting has a low ratio between highlight and shadow and thus allows all of the tones to be shifted upward without disastrously washing out the highlights. If you are taking a highlight and shadow reading with the camera's spot meter or a handheld meter you would want the lighting arranged so that the difference between the readings was only one stop or less. You would then overexpose the film when making the exposures. With the Olympus IS cameras, you can easily bracket the exposures with the exposure compensation control.

The opposite type of photography from high-key is low-key. In this case, the entire tonal range of the photograph is shifted so that blacks and dark tones predominate. In contrast to the above, there are few photos which benefit from a total low-key effect, it is usually more satisfactory to have at least some areas highlighted to bring them out against the overall dark tone of the photo. For this type of photograph I prefer to have a generally flat lighting ratio just as in high-key, but with one subject or parts of the subject highlighted by a direct light. Outdoors this can be a shaft of sunlight on a cloudy day. In the studio, it can be a spotlight or a broad light controlled by barn doors (folding panels which block off parts of the light). Portraits sometimes benefit from an effect in which the background and parts of the subject except for the face are low-key and the face alone is lighted normally. This is difficult to do outdoors, but can be accomplished by putting the subject in natural shade and using a reflector to throw light just where it is wanted. Homemade reflectors may be made from cardboard covered with crumpled aluminum foil. Another handy reflector is a double sided makeup mirror, the flat side can be used for general fill light and the magnifying mirror side can be used like a spotlight to throw a concentrated beam of light where it is needed. A friend or assistant is generally needed for this type of work to position and hold the reflector. Or a resourceful photographer can usually rig something up with a stand and some clamps.

Great Photos with Your Olympus IS Camera

The best way to get to know your camera is to spend as much time as you can actually taking photographs. As you get comfortable using the camera, you will find that all of the operations which seemed complex when you first read about them are actually simple and direct. Taking lots of pictures will let you see what you can do with these very flexible cameras and explore all of their capabilities. After all, film is still the cheapest thing in photography, so don't be afraid to experiment. It will be money well spent.

Selecting the Right Film

The ISO System

The International Standards Organization has now combined two older systems into the current ISO scheme. In this system, sensitivities set in the old ASA and DIN systems were retained, but the two were simply combined. Thus a film which formerly had an ASA of 100 and a DIN of 21° would have an ISO of 100/21°. Photographers and camera manufacturers never really took to this system, so it is highly unusual to find a camera today (except those still made in Germany!) with the DIN scale. Like most cameras, the Olympus IS series refers to film speed using the first half of the number only. However, most film packages use the complete designation.

ASA stands for American Standards Association, and uses a simple, arithmetic progression in which halving a number means the film has half the sensitivity and doubling a number means double the sensitivity. The second system is that of the Deutsche Industrie Norm (DIN), which is based on the premise that each increase of one in the number is a 1/3 stop increase in sensitivity. Thus a film with a DIN rating of 21° is 1/3 stop faster than one with a rating of 20°.

Film speed: This sensitivity of film to light is often referred to as film speed. More sensitive films require less light for proper expo-

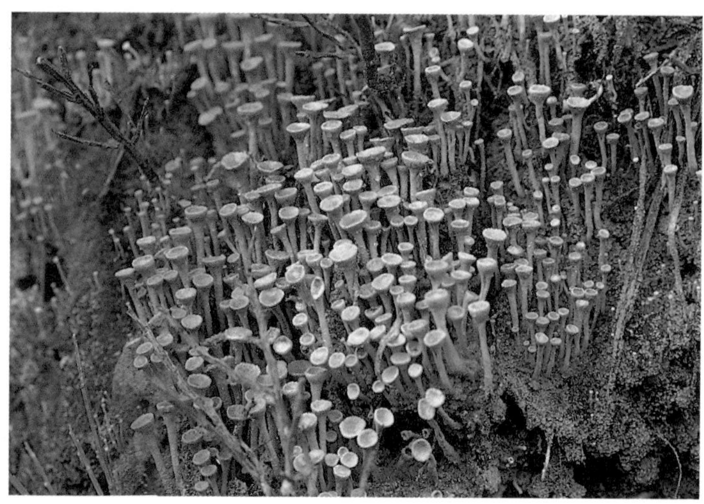

For photographs of subjects with intricate details, choose a slow film, such as ISO 25 for its fine grain structure.

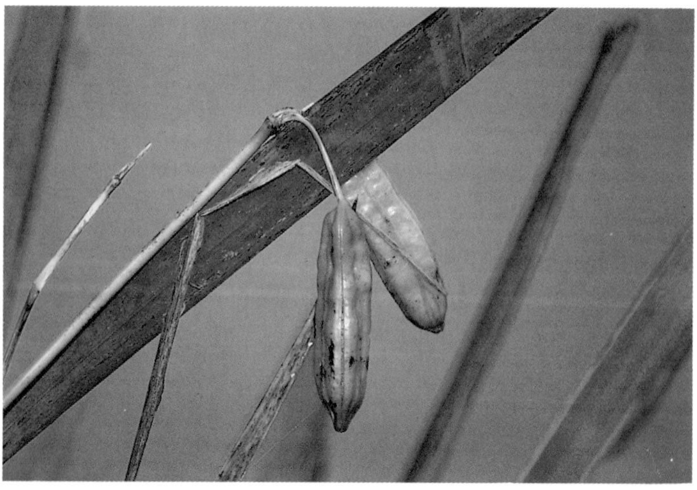

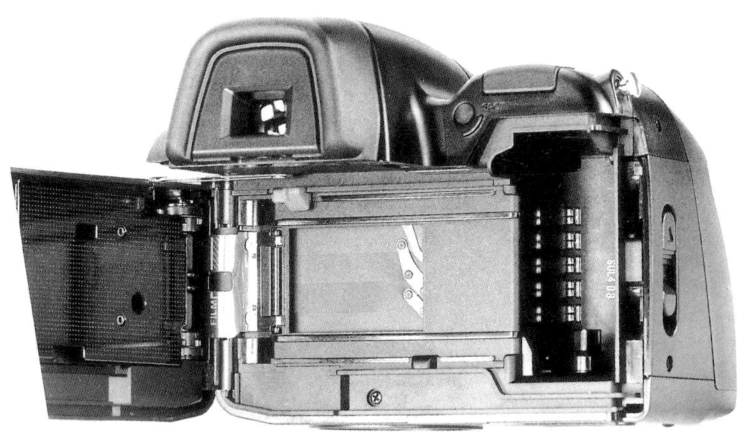

The open back of the Olympus IS-2 showing the chamber for the 35mm film cassette with the sensors that read the DX coded ISO film speed.

sure and have higher ISO ratings. The less light the film requires, the "faster" the film is considered to be. However, the term "fast film" applies to those with an ISO of 400 or higher. "Slower" films with less sensitivity have a lower ISO number and require more light for proper exposure. "Slow films" are generally those with an ISO of less than 100.

This would seem to argue for using a fast film all the time, but there are trade-offs. On a sunny day, there may be too much light to use very fast films. Also, as film speed increases, so does the film's grain size and it becomes more apparent as an image is enlarged. Color quality and saturation decrease as film speed increases. If bright, vibrant, sharp images are desired, use slower speed films. However, slow films have drawbacks also. They present more constraints on shutter speed and aperture selection. Using longer shutter speeds will allow more light to hit the film, but then a tripod is usually needed to prevent camera shake. Generally a medium speed film will be adequately sensitive for most photography, and will yield very high-quality results. As a general rule, use ISO 100 film outdoors in bright sun and ISO 200 and 400 on overcast days or indoors with flash.

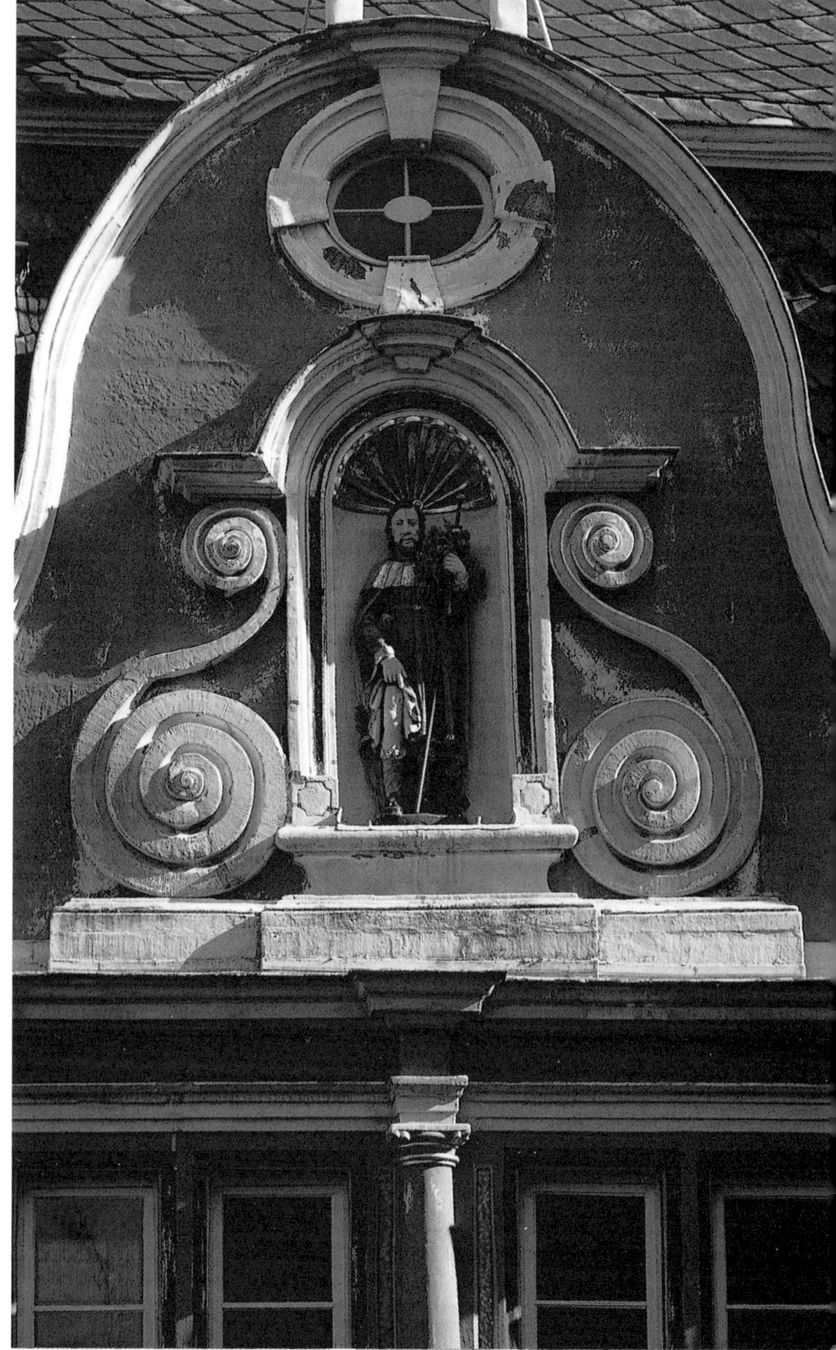

DX Coding

Olympus IS cameras are designed for use with DX coded film cassettes only. These cassettes have a coded pattern of conductive metal and non-conductive black paint on the back side which presses against electrical contacts inside the camera. This system informs the camera of the film's ISO when it has been loaded. Today, almost all films have DX coded cassettes. Non-DX coded film will be read as ISO 32. Exposure compensation (IS-2 and IS-3 only) can be used to correct the ISO setting up to ISO 200.

Film Processing

When traveling outside the United States, you may encounter some unusual films. Remember that processing may not be standard and it may be impossible to have the films processed at home. Film manufacturers everywhere are adopting the standard E-6 process for their color slide film and the C-41 process for their color negative film, but until this transition is complete be wary of unfamiliar films. This is unlikely to be a problem with black and white films, since they are reasonably standard no matter where they are made, but color films are another matter entirely. Because you can't know the quality and storage conditions of films bought during travel, it is far better to bring all the film you'll need with you and return with it for processing.

Any film which is marked "Process E-6" can be processed by any lab which processes Ektachrome, while any film marked "Process C-41" can be processed by any lab which processes normal color negative films.

Black and White Films

Almost every manufacturer of film makes some type of black and white film, and in many cases they make several varieties. In spite of the great diversity of brands and names, there are really only two sorts of black and white films available today. These are the traditional silver-based films and chromogenic film (currently made only by Ilford).

The IS camera's zoom lens offers a range of focal lengths for versatile compositions. Use the telephoto setting to "get close" to interesting architectural details.

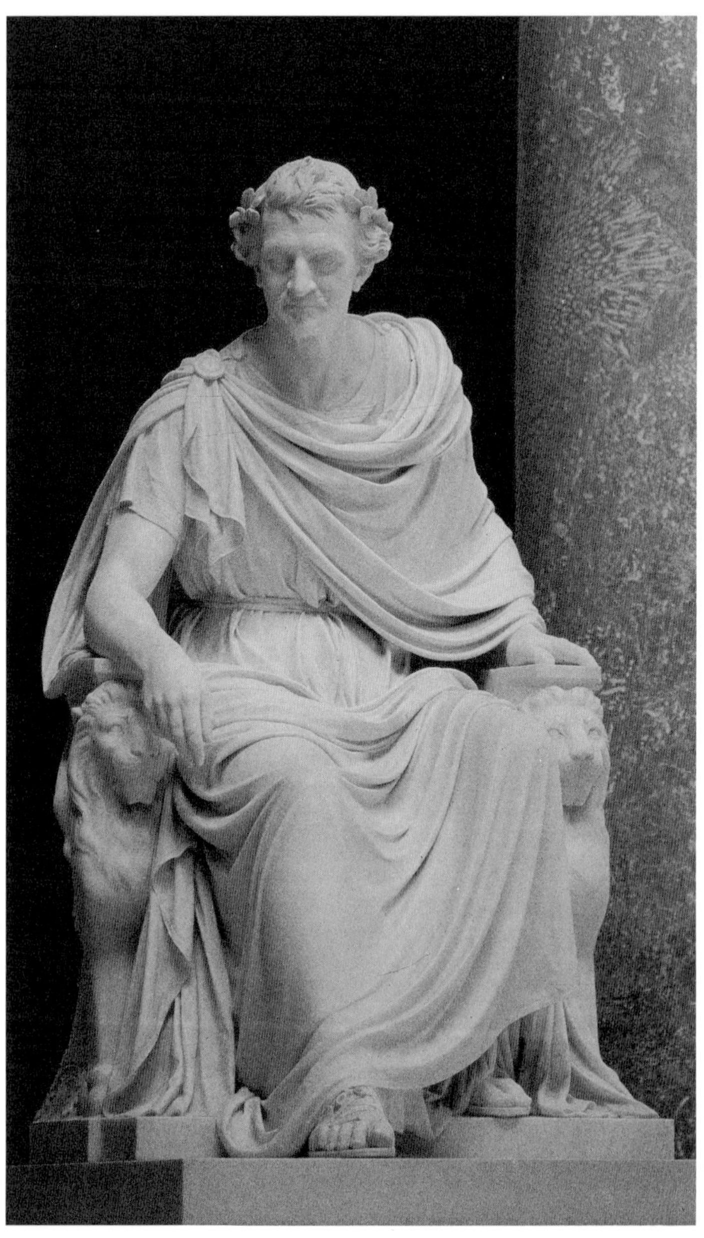

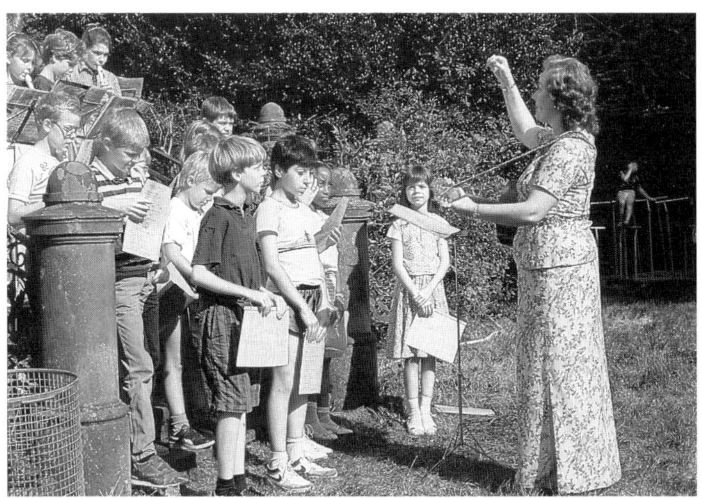

Black and white films have long been used for school photos. In this case, a medium speed film was selected which produced fine grain, excellent resolution and a broad tonal range.

In the standard types of silver-based films, the light sensitive agents in the film emulsion are silver compounds. After the full processing cycle, the image retained in the film is made up of tiny grains of metallic silver. Such emulsions were the first type of photographic material which produced a negative image from a positive one. The Daguerreotype, the very first process, made one-of-a-kind positive images which could not easily be reproduced. Today we benefit from films in which the sensitivity of the silver compounds has been greatly increased, the color sensitivity has been expanded to approximate the visible spectrum, and the size of the fully processed silver grains greatly reduced.

The chromogenic black and white films currently have only one representative, Ilford's XP-2. This film starts out much the same as a standard black and white film, but in addition it has color dye couplers linked-up with the light sensitive silver compounds in the emulsion. After exposure, the film is processed to

As evidenced by the slightly increased grain structure in the photograph, this sculpture was photographed in low light inside a building using a higher speed black and white film.

produce metallic silver grains. Then the dye couplers produce clouds of dye around these grains, and developed and undeveloped silver is completely removed from the film. Thus a processed negative on XP-2 contains no silver at all; the image is made entirely of tiny dye clouds. The benefit of the chromogenic film is that it is processed using C-41 (standard color negative) chemistry. This makes it much more convenient to find a photofinisher. For traditional black and white films, photographers usually process and print their own pictures.

Color Films

Modern color films come in two basic types; those in which the developed film yields a negative image, and those in which it yields a positive image. Color negative films are used to produce prints as the end result. The positive images produced by transparency films are called slides or chromes and are usually the end result themselves. Prints can also be made from slides, however, it is a more involved process.

Color Transparency Film

Color transparency films are generally distinguished from other films by having the suffix "chrome" as part of their names, as in Fujichrome, Agfachrome, Kodachrome, Ektachrome, etc. The films mentioned are registered trademarks of Fuji, Agfa, and Eastman Kodak respectively. Today, there are three types of color transparency films generally available, distinguished by how they are processed.

Kodachrome films from Kodak are direct descendents of the first commercially successful color film, the original Kodachrome. Kodachrome films are unique in that they are essentially multilayer black and white films. Through an extremely complex developing process, colored dyes are added sequentially to the layers of the emulsion to build up the full color image. Because of the difficulties involved, Kodachrome processing is being done by fewer and fewer labs. In spite of the inconvenience of finding processing, Kodachrome film is still the choice of many professionals for its color reproduction and archival qualities.

Black and white film was selected for this photograph because it enhanced the starkness of the cold winter landscape. ⇨

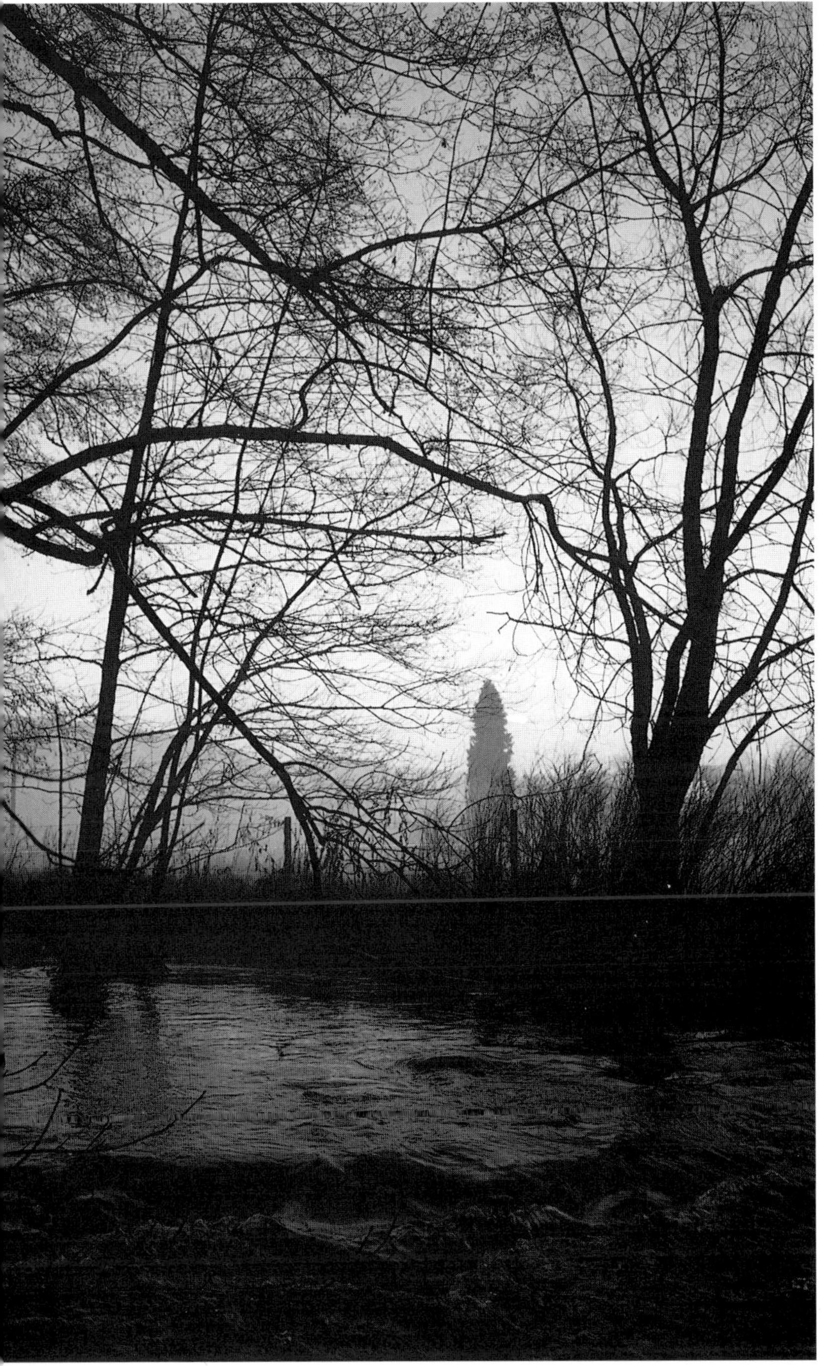

All other current color transparency films have dyes added as color couplers during the manufacturing process. Chemicals in the developing process react with the couplers to produce the dyes, giving these films their name, chromogenic (color generating). Almost all films in this category today are developed using the E-6 process pioneered by Kodak or its equivalent by Fuji, Agfa or others. Except for Kodachrome, most transparency films you are likely to encounter today will likely be E-6 compatible.

Using color transparency film: As a general rule, color transparency films have a relatively limited exposure range. This means they are very sensitive to incorrect exposure. For professional results, this range is limited to less than one stop of over- or underexposure. Properly exposing film with such a limited range requires a very precise exposure meter and careful metering technique. When working with the Olympus IS cameras, the metering system is very accurate and I have come to trust it in almost all situations. In working with transparency films, the spot meter can be a very valuable tool, so pay particular attention to learning to use it properly.

Generally, color transparency films will tolerate underexposure better than overexposure, and many photographers habitually underexpose the film by as much as 1/3 to 1/2 stop. This darkens the image just enough to produce more saturated colors. The photographer should be very familiar with exposure techniques and the film being used for the best results.

Recently there has been somewhat of a revival in color transparency films, with some wonderful new films coming along from most of the major manufacturers. It is fun to experiment with different slide films from different manufacturers as each has its own characteristics and color rendition. However, most amateur photographers today tend to use color print film exclusively. They want a final product which can be easily duplicated and viewed without the hassle of setting up a slide projector.

The pillars and shadows act as interesting compositional elements in this asymmetrical landscape photo. ➪

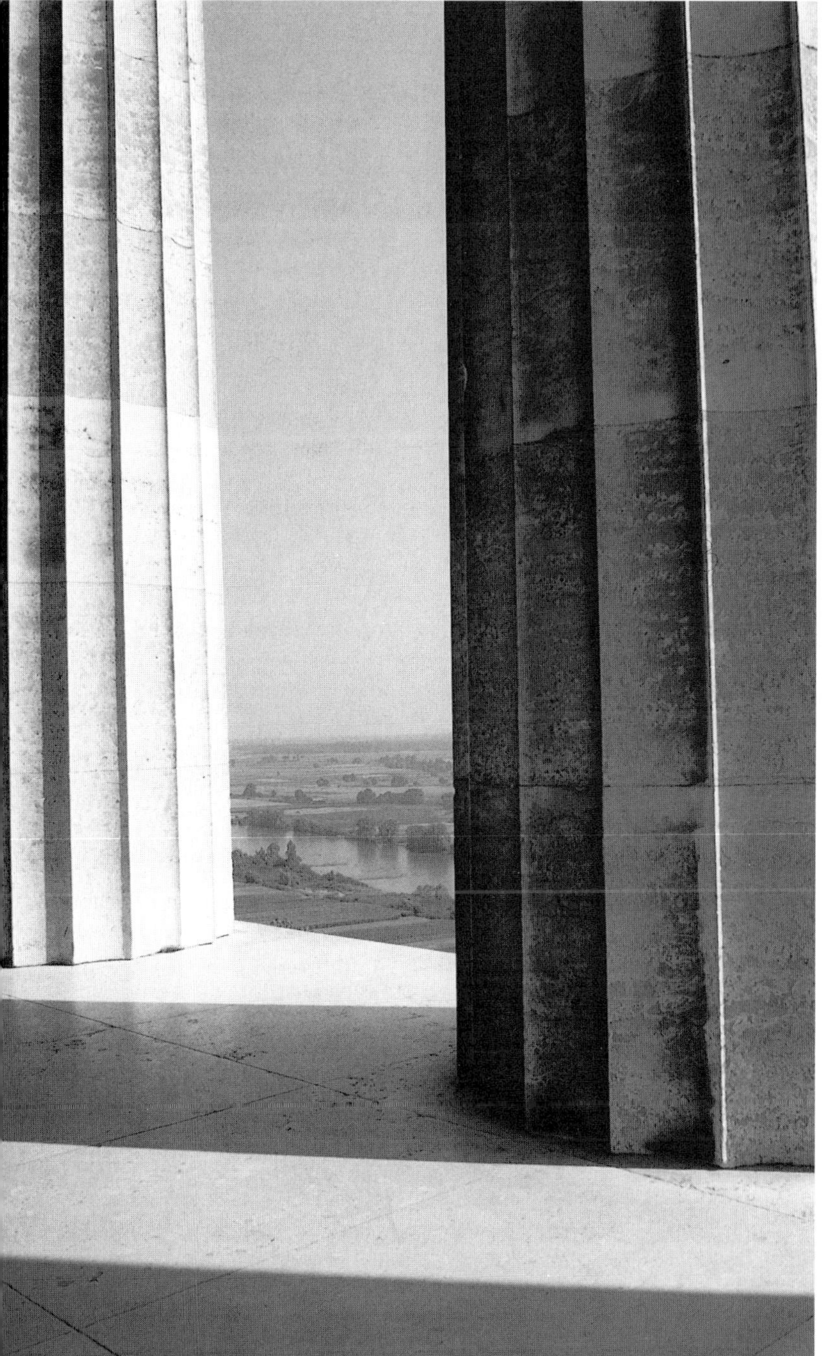

Color Negative Film

Color print films are readily available in speeds ranging from ISO 25 up to ISO 3200. The same rules apply as with any other film, the lower the ISO number the finer the grain and the greater the resolving power to render fine detail. Generally speaking, the lower the ISO the higher the contrast. Also, different color films will reproduce color differently. There are a variety of "recipes" for film, and every manufacturer has its own. Some films are designed with a warmer color-balance to make skin-tones look good. Others make bright colors look more vibrant. In addition to film type, processing has a huge effect on how the final image looks. It is highly recommended you choose a lab that employs knowledgeable people to answer questions you may have about the quality of your photographs.

Color print films also come in two versions, amateur and professional. Do not be confused by this, the professional film does not necessarily provide better quality. It is simply more carefully matched to the needs of the professional, and should be stored in refrigeration to hold it at its peak color balance prior to exposure. Professional color films are issued on the assumption that the film will be exposed within a short time of removal from refrigeration, and then processed promptly. If you are the type who leaves film in the camera for months at a time, you probably should not use professional films.

Color Balance

Practically all color films you will encounter are designed for use with daylight or electronic flash, which is color-balanced to approximate daylight. Using these films under other lighting conditions will produce photographs with unnatural color rendition, even though the light source may appear "normal" to the human eye. Common fluorescent lighting gives photos a greenish cast. Ordinary household lighting is usually tungsten, and produces a warm, golden-yellow tint on daylight film. These colored tones can be used to advantage in certain situations, for example night shots benefit from the colors created by different artificial light sources. Also, artificial light sources can be used to great effect in combination with natural light or electronic flash. For information on color compensation when exposing color films under various types of lighting, see the "Filters" section in this chapter.

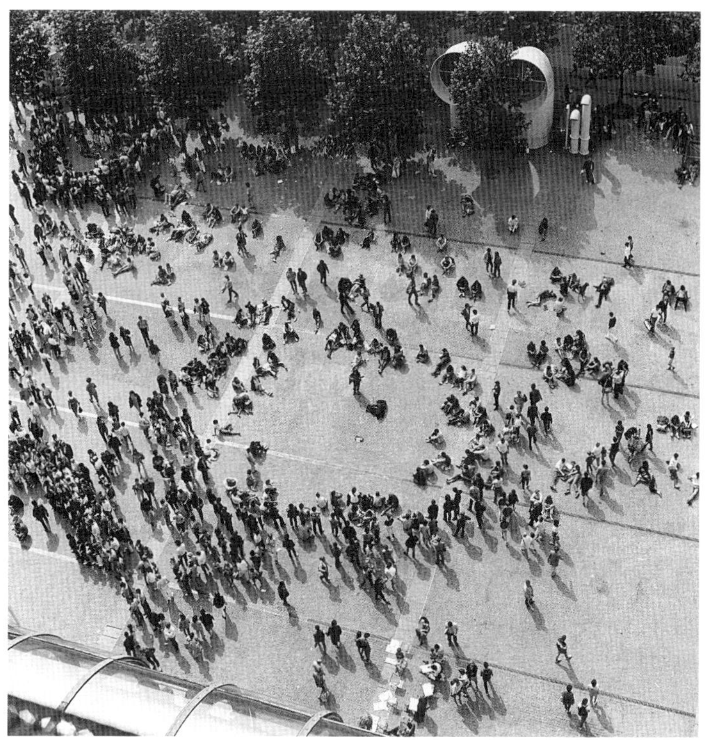

When photographed from a bird's-eye view, a crowd of people looks more like a pattern in this public square. Photo: Paul Comon

Composition

Ultimately the composition and content can overrule all other factors and determine the final success of a photo. If a picture is perfectly exposed but badly composed, it is just as worthless as if it suffered some other obvious technical flaw.

While a sense of composition is innate in certain people, I feel that everyone can learn enough to at least get by. If you conscientiously study composition, it will begin to become automatic and you will no longer have to work at it. This is just like learning to use your camera, learning to drive your car, or any other task which at first requires constant attention and thought. After a time it becomes so easy that you can not believe how difficult it was at first.

Although I have heard people pontificate about "esthetic rules", I personally feel that anyone who insists that there are such rules is a fool. The only real rule is whether the picture works, and by that I do not necessarily mean that it has to be pleasing to the eye. What is important is that the photographer had a specific compositional intent and was able to carry it through to the finished photograph. This section on composition is the distillation of my own experience, and must not be considered as anything more than suggestions. You should consider them, and then use or discard as they apply or do not apply to your personal photography.

Proportion

One thing I must get out of the way right at the beginning is something called aspect ratio. This is simply the ratio of the short sides of a rectangle to the long sides. A problem which you will frequently encounter in working with 35mm is that the aspect ratio is somewhat long; that is 1:1-1/2. The dimensions of a 35mm negative are 24 x 36 mm or roughly 1 x 1-1/2 inches. This is close to the aspect ratio which the ancient Greeks considered ideal, and referred to as the "golden rectangle". It is certainly a pleasing aspect ratio and many commonly encountered objects maintain approximately this ratio.

The problem comes about when we try to make prints from our 35mm negatives. Most of the common print sizes do not have the same aspect ratio; for example the common sizes of photographic paper are (in inches) 8 x 10, 11 x 14, 14 x 17, and 16 x 20. All of these have an aspect ratio of approximately 1:1-1/4. You can easily see that enlarging a negative with an aspect ratio of 1:1-1/2 onto a sheet of paper with an aspect ratio of 1:1-1/4 causes problems. You always lose a bit off the long dimension. You may solve this in several ways. The first is to order special 8 x 12 prints which some photofinishers now supply and then compose the photo exactly in the viewfinder. The other solution is to allow for this slight cutoff at either end when composing the picture in the camera. The last possibility is to ignore it altogether and face the prospect of cutting Aunt Julia in half when taking a group family portrait! The important thing is to be aware of the difference in proportion so that you will not be surprised by it later.

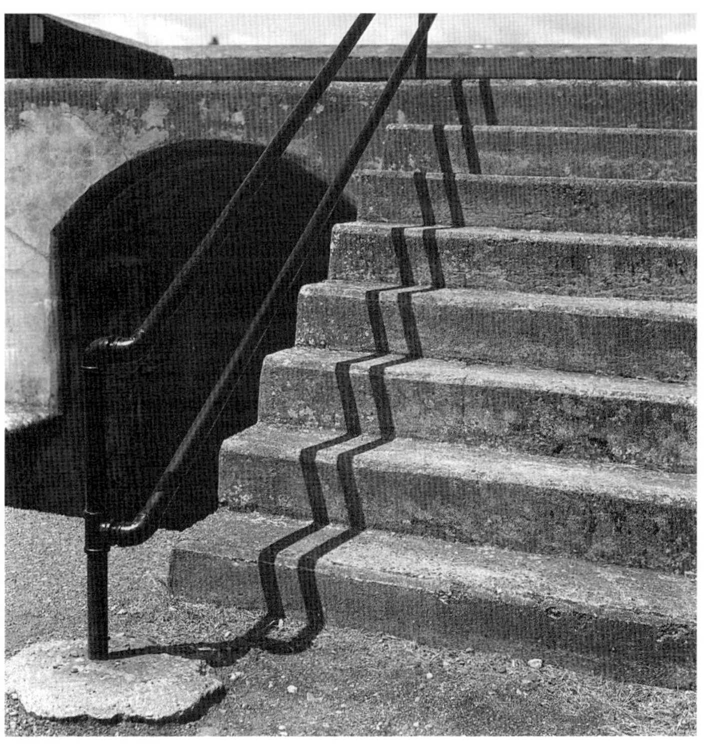

The diagonal lines in this photograph lead the viewer's eye right up the stairs. Photo: Paul Comon

Now let's get to the meat of the matter. All of us who have learned to read in Western cultures have learned to scan the page from left to right, starting at the top and working down. This is learned so early that we are not generally aware of it, but it carries over into our viewing of photographs and other art. We tend to start our viewing of an image on the left side and scan across to the right. We will typically start toward the top. Our eye enters at the upper left and scans across and, if it is not stopped by anything it tends to just keep on going right out of the picture. You will find that many photos also have this effect on your eyes and that these are usually the ones which do not hold your attention. The eye must be held in the frame, either by a border of some sort or by the interest of the subject itself.

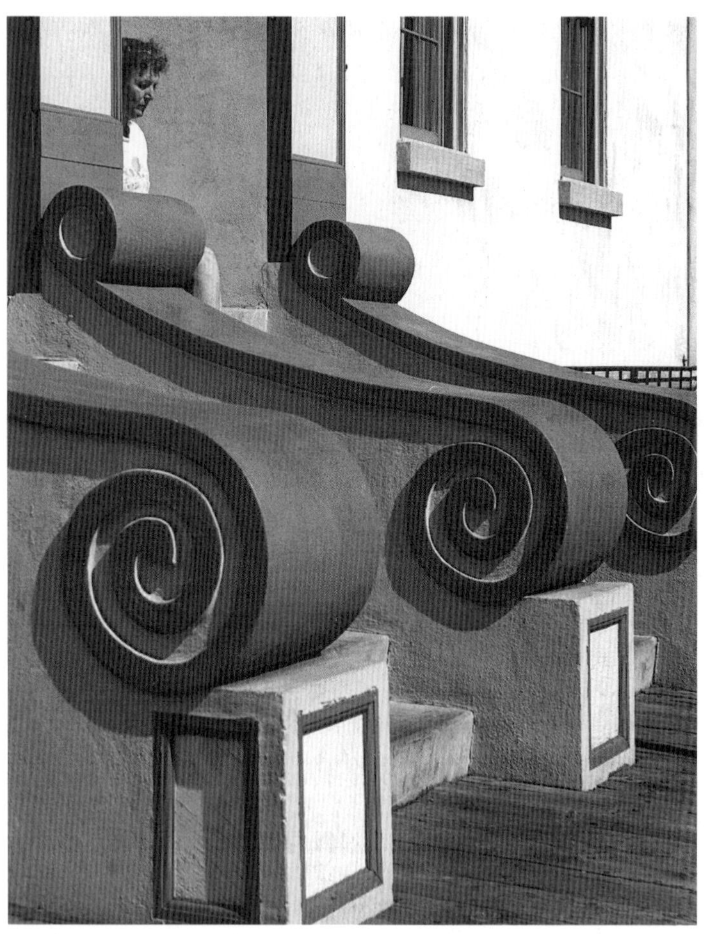

These unusual stair railings create an eye-catching pattern and the woman in the doorway adds a unexpected element to make the viewer look a little longer. Photo: Paul Comon

The Rule of Thirds

Beginning photographers usually have the habit of putting the main subject at dead center, and this tendency is accentuated by autofocus cameras which will focus on the subject in the center. Make use of the focus lock feature and rearrange your composi-

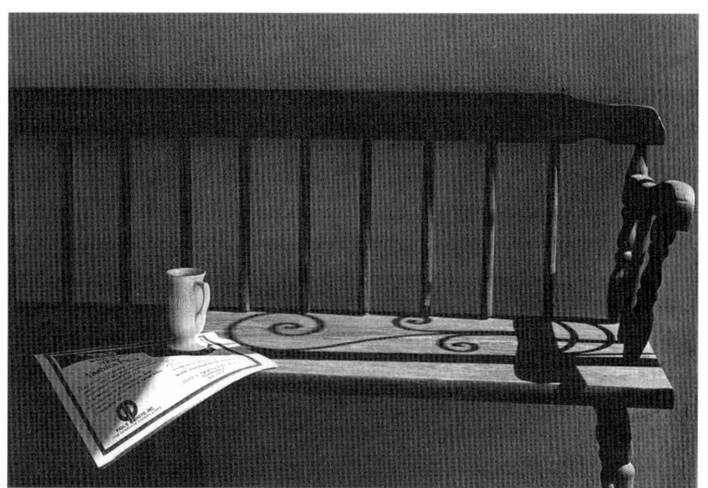

Sidelighting from early morning or late afternoon sunlight can create an interesting photograph from even the most mundane domestic scene. Photo: Paul Comon

tion. Do not leave everything at the center, your photos will be terribly boring if you do. The best places to put your main subject are generally positions obtained by the rule of thirds. If you divide the frame into thirds and place the subject along the line which divided the image into 2/3, 1/3 you will usually find this placement produces an interesting photo.

Here I have divided a "golden rectangle" similar in proportion to a 35mm frame into thirds on each axis. Locating your main subject along one of these lines will generally be the best placement and locating it at the intersection of two of the lines is usually even better. Of course not all subjects lend themselves to this sort of placement. There are many other arrangements which will produce visually interesting compositions. Two which are frequently used are the S curve and the pyramid. In the S curve the planes of the subject are arranged in a gentle curve with the first bend in the curve at about the 1/3 down line and sweeping through broad arcs to the bottom. This composition works especially well with figure studies. The pyramid works well when you are dealing with groups of asymmetrical subjects, such as groups

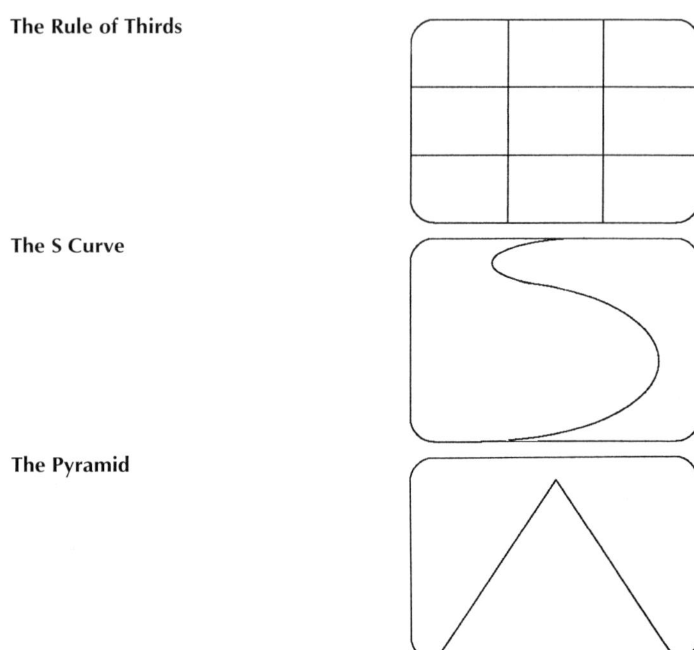

of people. By putting the tallest person in the middle and others around that person such an arrangement may be created.

One of the best ways to study composition and form is to get several books on the old masters. These great painters worked out these same principles of composition hundreds of years ago, and put them through infinite permutations. Don't be afraid to steal compositional ideas from the masters, you certainly won't be the first! And, most important of all, don't be afraid to break the rules. For every suggestion I have made above there will be pictorial situations in which just the opposite of what I have said will work better. Therefore, the best advice I can give is, "Practice, experiment, break all the rules and learn."

Photographic Design

When composing potential photographs, it is helpful to ask what makes an image interesting. Think about what initially attracted you to a subject and try to capture that same appeal in your photographs. A benefit of the IS-series cameras' automatic features is that technically excellent photographs can be made with very little effort. By letting the camera control exposure and focus, the photographer is free to concentrate on the subject and composition in a picture.

Listed are just a few of the elements which have been employed in all the visual arts to draw the viewer's interest. Look for ways to incorporate them into your photographs for better results.

Detail: Crop in close to eliminate distractions. You can often say more about a subject by showing only a limited view. Decide what it is you want to portray in a photograph and examine the small details that describe that aspect of your subject.

Line: Line can be used to bring viewers into your photographs or lead them to points of interest. Horizontal and vertical lines are static and impart a sense of immobility. Diagonal lines are dynamic and provide a sense of movement and vitality. Rather than shoot a subject straight on, position yourself at an angle to the subject or even try tipping the camera.

Lighting: Photography is about recording the light reflected off an object. Of course, different types of light do not produce the same effects. The quality of natural light is entirely different at noon and six o'clock in the evening. And this is why it is a challange to make fill flash lighting look natural.

A photograph can be enhanced by lighting a subject appropriately. Sidelighting brings out texture and surface detail. Backlighting accentuates the shape and form of an object. Light can also be the subject of a photograph; the pattern produced by sunlight through a lace curtain or the shadow cast by an ornate iron fence.

Pattern: Pattern is so common in the world around us that we often fail to notice it, but isolated in a photograph, the repetition of a shape or form becomes a striking image. Be alert to the presence of natural and manmade patterns, such as a picket fence, a row of trees or produce lined up at a farmer's market.

Viewpoint: Try a different point of view for photographs that grab peoples' attention. When photographing kids and pets, shoot at

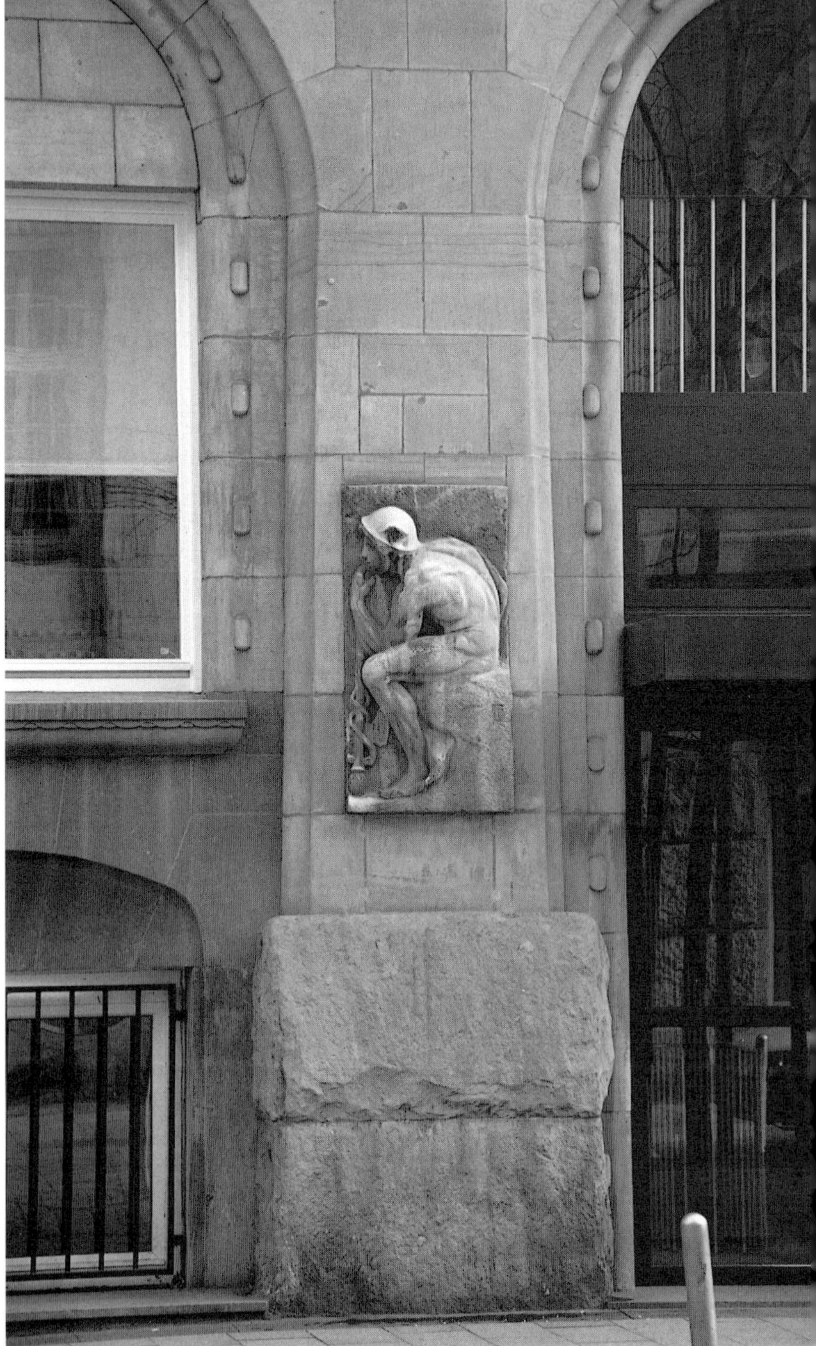

their level, rather than looking down at them. Show your subject from an angle that no one has ever seen it before. To make on object seem to tower over the camera, shoot up at it.

Filters

Filters are devices which alter the light passing through the lens in specific ways. Most commonly filters are round pieces of optically flat glass mounted in metal rings and attached to the lens by the threads inside the front rim of the lens. Some filters common today are square or rectangular and are held in special frames which screw onto the front of the lens. The third type of filters are called gelatin filters or gels and are thin sheets of colored gelatin or plastic and are used in certain lenses by way of a special holder which fits onto the front of the lens. Regardless of which type of filter you decide to use you must buy the filter or filter holder in the correct size for your camera. The IS-1 and IS-2 cameras require a 49mm size, the IS-3 requires a 55mm size and the IS-10 requires a 52mm size. Filters and filter systems are available at all well-stocked camera shops.

Filters are image modifiers. They can be divided into three main categories; those used primarily with black and white films, those used primarily with color films and those which can be used with any sort of film.

Filters for Black and White Photography

The primary use for filters in black and white photography is to selectively lighten or darken the gray tones in which colors are rendered. The primary colors of light are red, green and blue. By mixing them, all colors can be produced. Adding equal parts of all three produces white light. The secondary colors of light are cyan, magenta, and yellow. (Yes, I know that your school art teacher told you that the primary colors were red, yellow and blue. The teacher was wrong.)

⇦ This photo seems to break the rules of composition by placing the object of interest directly in the center of the photograph. However, the symmetry of the arches on either side of the relief sculpture add interest and a dynamic element to the photograph.

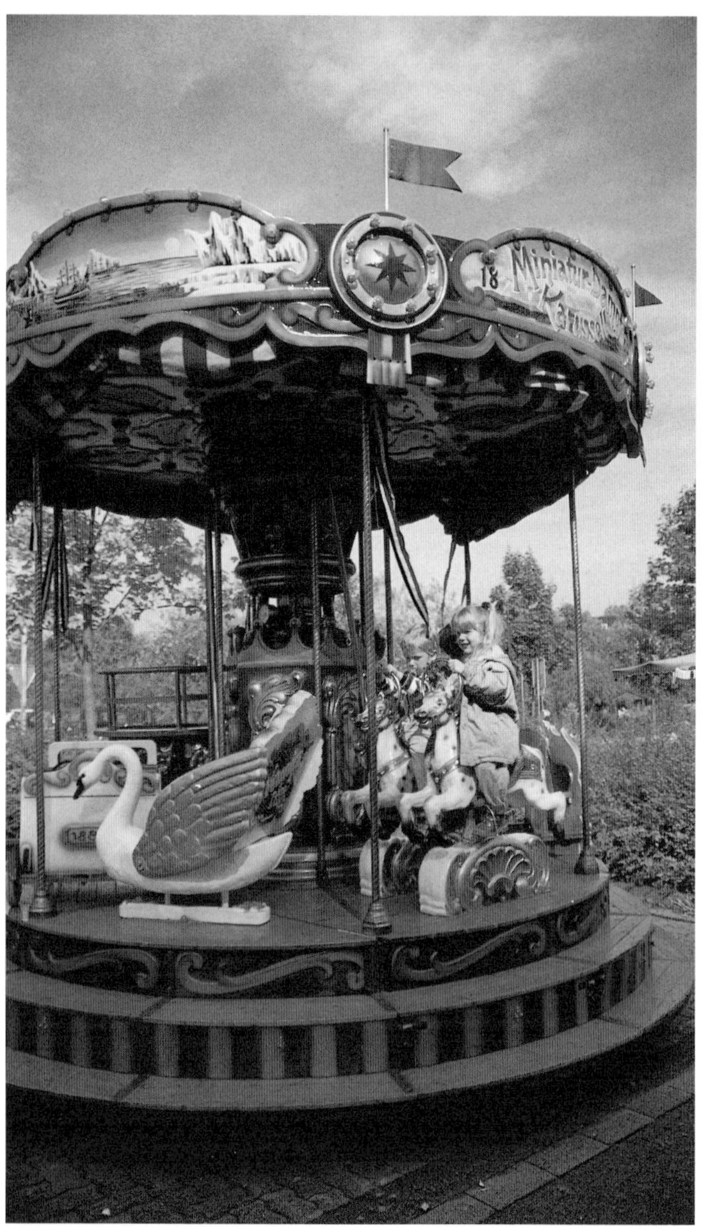
18
Miniatur-
Karussell

For our purposes in this discussion we need go into this no more deeply. If you wish to learn more about color theory, there are many good books on color photography and printing which explain this in detail.

A filter of a particular color will pass wavelengths of the same color of light and will absorb other colors. Thus a red filter will pass red light and absorb both green and blue. In a black and white photograph, a red subject shot through a red filter will be rendered lighter than without the filter, and both blue and green subjects will be rendered darker. Knowing this can be useful when you need to separate colors into tones in black and white photography. As a specific example, let's consider an apple tree full of ripe, red fruit. If you photograph the tree on black and white film without using any filter, the red apples and green foliage will be rendered about the same shade of gray and there is little differentiation between the two. However, if you use a red filter to photograph the same tree the red apples will be rendered lighter and the green foliage darker and they will be well differentiated in the print.

Perhaps you do not like this effect, thinking that the light rendering of the apples and dark foliage is not very attractive. In this case you can create the opposite effect with a green filter. This will lighten the rendering of the foliage and darken the apples. In each case, remember that a filter will lighten its own and similar colors and darken the other colors. Also, the more saturated the color of the filter, the more pronounced its effect will be.

Basic filter types: Filters are made in a broad range of colors. These are just a few of the basics for a well outfitted black and white photographer.

Red: This filter, usually a Number 25, is useful for darkening blue skies to produce a dramatic effect when photographing clouds.

Yellow: Also usable to accentuate clouds against the sky, but will not darken the sky as much as the red filter above. Many land-

⇦ **The use of a yellow filter in this black and white snapshot is evidenced by the increased contrast in the sky and clouds. Without the filter the sky would have appeared almost white with the clouds barely visible.**

scape photographers use a yellow filter nearly all the time. If you want a compromise between the strong effect of the red filter and the lesser effect of the yellow you can use an orange filter.

Light green: This filter is very useful for de-emphasizing facial blemishes (as long as they are reddish) in portraiture. It will bring the tone of the blemishes much closer to the overall skin tone than would be the case in a photo taken with no filter.

UV (Ultraviolet): This filter is designed to absorb most UV light. In spite of the fact that optical glass in the lens absorbs almost all UV, some still gets through and can cause a haze, particularly in landscape photographs. This filter will help to reduce this haze. Since it is otherwise photographically neutral, many photographers leave one of these filters on the front of each of their lenses at all times as a protection against damage. It is far cheaper to replace a cracked or scratched filter than to replace a lens. Consider these filters cheap insurance.

Filters for Color Photography

The above filters for black and white can only be used with color films when a photo with an overall color cast is desired. Filters used with color films are almost all designed to correct for imbalances in the color rendition of the film caused by a mismatch between the light source and the film type.

Conversion Filters for Color Film

Light Source	**Daylight or Electronic Flash**	**Photolamp (3400K)**	**Tungsten Lamp (3200K)**
Film Type			
Daylight	No Filter	80B	80A
Tungsten Type A	85	No Filter	82A
Tungsten Type B	85B	81A	No Filter

FL filters: These filters are used to attempt to get a pleasing color rendition of subjects which must be photographed under fluorescent lighting. Unfortunately, even the best filter is not always successful in this situation since a filter can only block or subtract light. It can not supply colors of light which are not there in the first place. Most types of fluorescent tubes are deficient in red light and no amount of filtration can supply the red which is simply missing. If you have no choice and must take color photographs under fluorescent light, the FL-D filter is the one you would use if you are working with Daylight type film. The FL-B is the one to use with Tungsten type film.

80 series: When working with photoflood lamps or other tungsten light sources and daylight film, these filters will allow you to balance the light to the film. While the color rendition may not be perfect, it will generally be pleasing and accurate enough for non-critical applications. If you are using standard photoflood or photopearl lamps which have a color temperature of 3200°K you should use the 80A filter with daylight film. If you are working with certain types of photographic lamps which have a color temperature of 3400°K then you will have to use the 80B filter with these films. Although the color temperature of ordinary household incandescent lamps varies considerably, it is generally lower than that of photo lamps. Using the 80A filter will generally produce a pleasing if slightly warm effect with these lights.

Skylight 1A and 1B: These filters are basically the same as the UV filters mentioned above for black and white films but with the addition of a slight pink tint to give an overall warming effect which many photographers find pleasing. The 1B has more of a warming effect than the 1A. When taking photos of people this helps to give the appearance of a warm, healthy glow. Skylight filters may be left on the lens all the time as general protection.

General Purpose Filters

Polarizing filter: This is a very interesting filter which has uses for many types of photography. As you probably remember from physics class, light has both wave and particle properties, but it is the wave properties which concern us most as photographers. Natural daylight and light from most other sources is said to be unpolarized, which means that the waves are undulating in all directions about the axis of travel. A polarizing filter removes all of the light which is not undulating in a particular plane, and the light which passes through it is said to be polarized. Since the polarizing filter is usually mounted in a rotating ring, it may be turned to selectively block out light which has already been polarized in a particular plane.

This is important in photography because many natural forms of polarized light exist and by selectively blocking them, a greater degree of control over the final photograph can be achieved. Because much of the light which causes atmospheric haze is naturally polarized these filters may be used in both black and white and color photography to darken blue skies and emphasize clouds by removing this haze. This effect will vary with the angle of the sun and time of day, being greatest when the sun is at more of an angle to the filter. By turning the filter while looking through the viewfinder, the filter can easily be adjusted for maximum effect.

The other common use for polarizing filters is the reduction or elimination of reflections from shiny surfaces. All shiny surfaces (except polished metal) polarize the light as they reflect it, so by turning the filter while looking through the camera it is possible to "tune out" the reflections. If you don't want to eliminate the reflections entirely, you can adjust the filter to give them just the amount of emphasis you want. Reflections on water in a landscape photograph are an example of a situation in which you would want to de-emphasize the reflections without eliminating them entirely.

In color photography, a polarizing filter also will tend to give more saturated colors overall since it eliminates much of the polarized reflected light which reduces color saturation.

There are two types of polarizing filters but only one of them is really suitable for use with the IS cameras. Most older polarizers were of the linear type, passing light polarized only in one plane. Because the semi-silvered mirror used in the IS camera's autofocus system also polarizes the light sent to the autofocus sensor,

This study of a store window could not have been photographed without the use of a polarizing filter which eliminated the reflections caused by the window glass. ➪

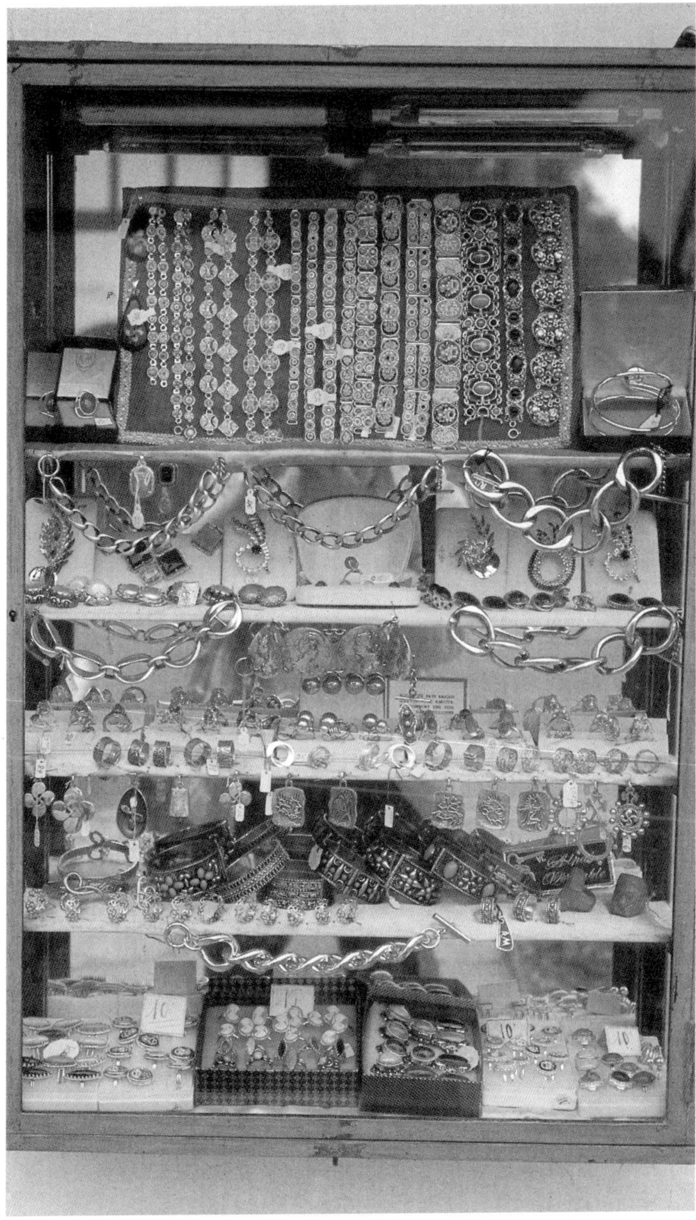

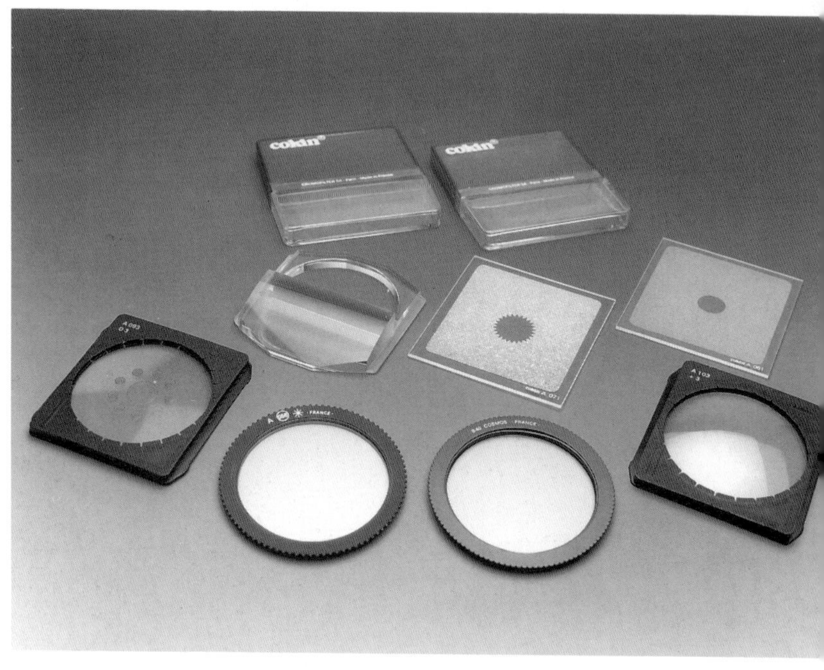

The Cokin Filter System® is one of the most popular ways of adding interesting effects to photographic images.

such a filter will prevent the autofocus system from working. To solve this problem a special type of polarizer called a circular polarizer has been developed. These pass some light in every orientation so they will not defeat the autofocus system. Circular polarizers do not produce as great an effect as linear polarizers, so many photographers still prefer the older type and will simply focus the camera manually when using the filter. With the IS-10, a polarizing filter may cause vignetting at the 28mm lens position. This can be minimized by selecting a filter with a thin mount.

The Cokin soft-focus filter used for this photograph of trees takes the image from mundane to interesting due to the mood that's created. ⇨

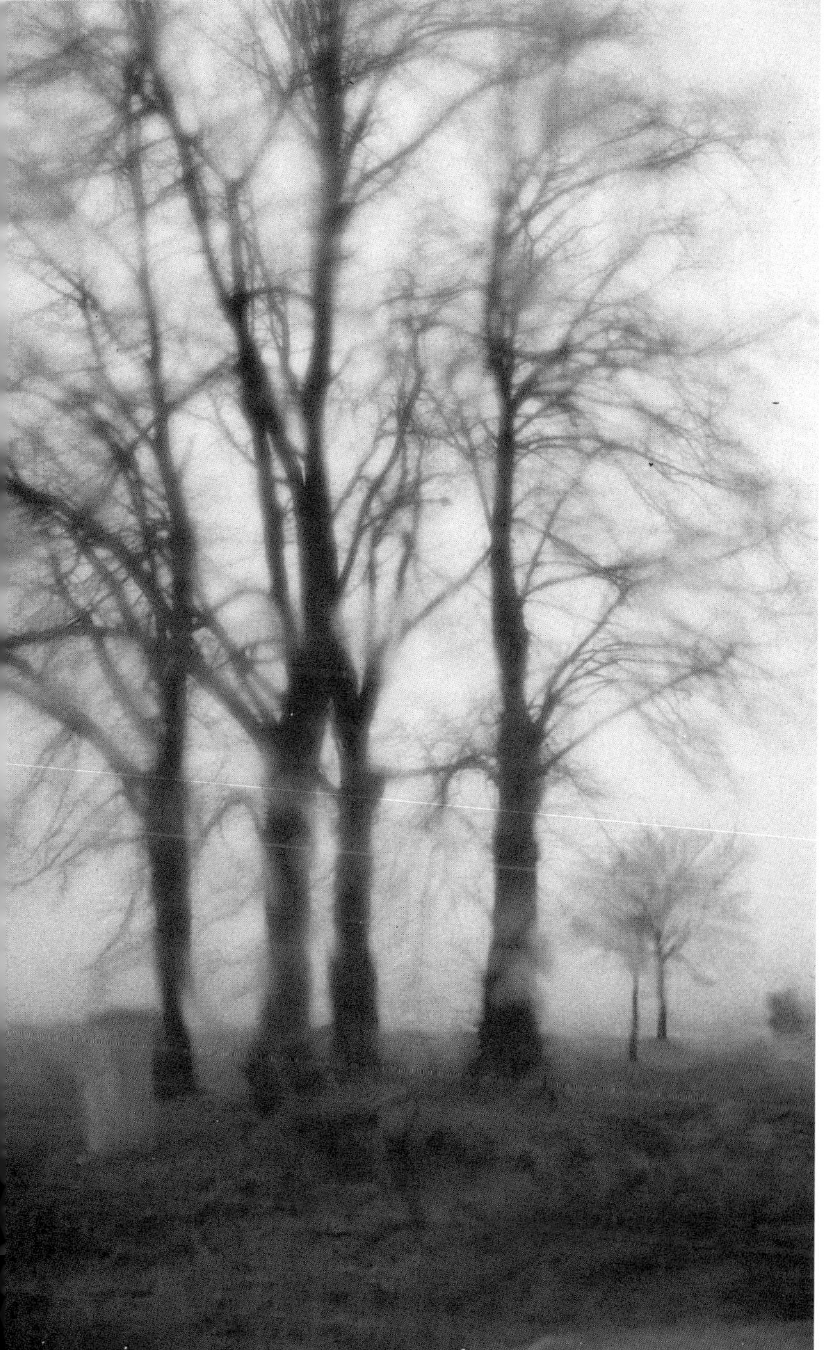

Special types of filters: There has been a recent increase in interest in filters of all types with the result that a number of new types have appeared. Foremost among these are the systems which utilize a holder which screws into the lens and square or rectangular filters. These filters are generally made from plastic, although a few glass ones do exist. There is not space here go into all of them in great detail, but I would like to mention a few which I have found to be particularly useful.

The graduated neutral density filters are designed so that they become gradually darker from one side to the other. They may be fitted into the holder and aligned so that the darker portion of the filter affects only part of the picture. Such a filter is very useful when a bright sky needs to be darkened without darkening the rest of the picture. They come in different values, different degrees of darkening effect. Additionally they come in colors, so by the use of one of them a colorless sky may be made blue, or whatever other color you desire.

Another type of filter for these holders is a colored sheet with a hole in the center. This can be used to color the background without coloring the central subject and may be used for a number of special effects in portraiture. Since the filter is held close to the front of the lens the outline of the hole is not rendered sharp but softly fades from colored to uncolored.

Diffusion filters also are a valuable addition to your filter lineup. These soften the finished photo and often enhance a portrait by softening the image. Diffusers also can add a certain mood to landscape and scenic shots.

It is important that you attach nothing to the front of your lens which will interfere with the focusing action or which will be so heavy that it produces unnecessary drag on the focusing mechanism. Bellows type lens hoods and other heavy accessories must never be used with the IS camera's lenses. A filter holder and one or two filters is not likely to cause harm, but I would avoid anything heavier.

Close-up Filters

If you find that you are frustrated because you cannot focus close enough with an IS lens, close-up filters are a good solution. These are simply magnifying lenses which are mounted in threaded rings like filters and screw into the front of the lens. The Olympus

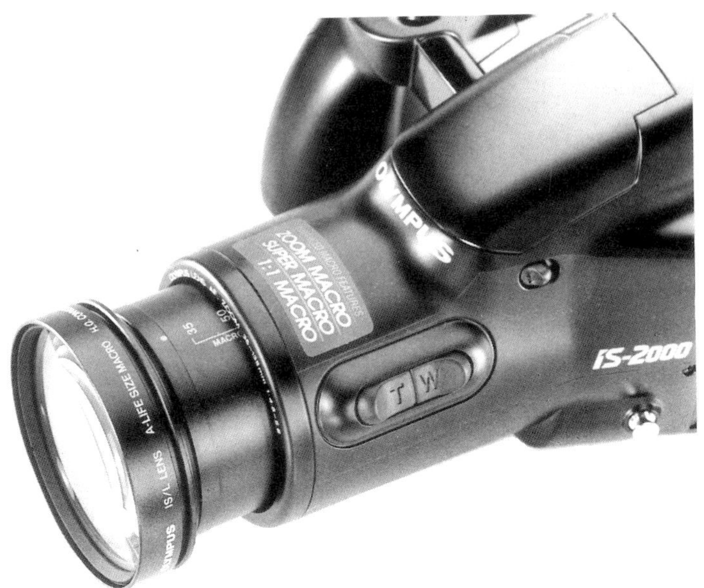

The IS-2 camera with the IS/L A-Life Size macro converter lens.

IS/L macro converters are special close-up lens designed to match the optical characteristics of the IS lenses, but you may wish to have the versatility of a variety of magnifications.

Although numerous firms make close-up filters, the cheapest ones are usually not of very high optical quality. Even the best will not equal the resolution of a true macro lens, but for general photography they are quite good. For the best possible image quality, it is not a good idea to use them with the lens set at the widest aperture. Stopping down two or three stops from wide open will provide much better quality.

Electronic Flash and Accessories

Electronic Flash Units

Before going into specific details about the Olympus G40 accessory flash unit, I would like to give you some advice and comments about electronic flash in general. An electronic flash is a device which produces a burst of very intense light for a very short period of time. This burst of light is produced by passing a high-voltage electric current through a gas-filled tube, called a discharge tube. The amount of light output by an electronic flash unit is determined by the amount of energy passed through the tube and its duration.

Modern electronic flash units are designed so that the flash exposure may be accurately controlled. This is accomplished by

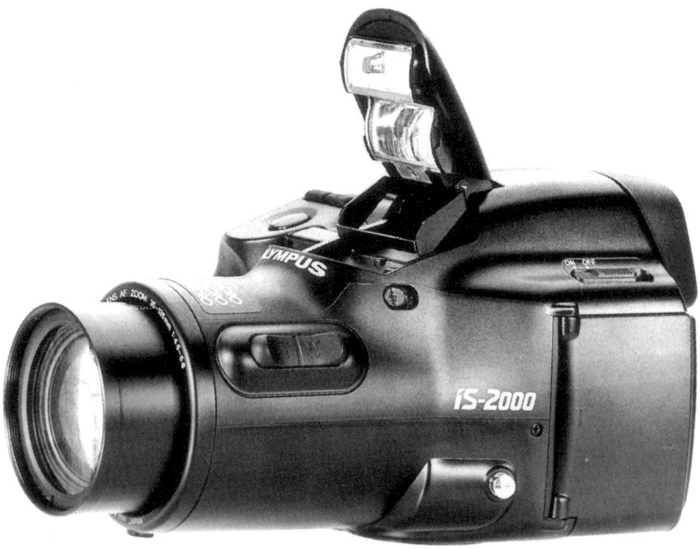

All the IS-series cameras have a built-in IVP (Intelligent Variable-Power) flash system. Simply activate the flash, and the camera selects the appropriate light output.

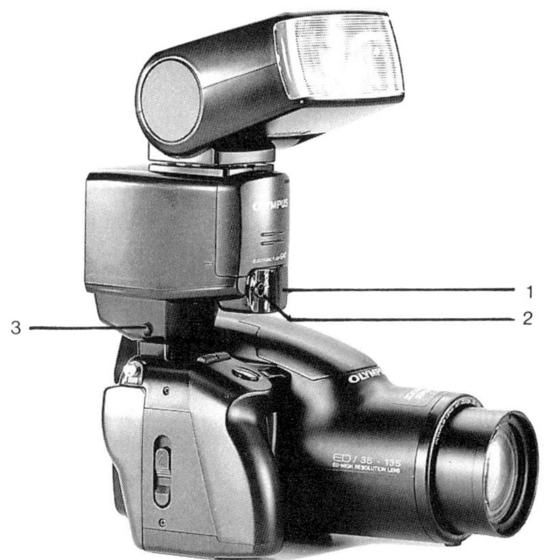

The IS-2 camera with an Olympus G40 flash unit.
1. Autofocus assist illuminator
2. Auto exposure flash sensor
3. Flash lock release (to remove the camera from the shoe mount)

a switching circuit which uses a special type of transistor called a Thyristor. This merely means that this type of flash unit has a variable output controlled by a switching circuit. There are two ways in which this switching circuit is commonly controlled to provide just the right amount of light for correct exposure. The first way is through a light sensor mounted on the flash which receives light reflected back from the subject and shuts off the discharge tube when it senses that the subject has received correct exposure. This is a generally accurate system, but it suffers from some drawbacks. With the light sensor integrated into the flash unit, it does not take into account the use of filters or different focal length lens settings.

To get around these problems, camera designers have mounted the sensor inside the camera just as they have done with TTL light meters. However, it is impractical to mount such a sensor in a position to pick up the light just after it passes through the lens. Designers have instead mounted the sensor so it points toward the film and picks up light reflected off the surface of the film during the exposure. These systems are referred to as Off The Film or OTF metering. Although mounting the sensor inside the camera eliminates having to set exposure compensation for such things as filters, it still suffers from the same problems as any other metering system which uses reflected light. Exposure settings are calculated for scenes of medium reflectance. Subjects which reflect too much or too little light will fool this system just as they fool the camera's ambient light meter.

Olympus has followed another route in designing the G40 flash unit. Flash duration is determined by the subject distance, and overall exposure is controlled by the flash duration and lens aperture. This system is not fooled by unusual subject reflectance, and is therefore much more accurate than flash systems which use reflected light to determine exposure.

The Olympus G40 is a fully dedicated electronic flash designed for use with IS-series cameras except the IS-10. A dedicated flash unit is one which interfaces with the camera to exchange data with the camera's electronic systems. When attached to the flash shoe on top of the camera's handgrip, the G40 will operate in all of the flash modes to be described here.

Flash Modes

Auto Mode

The built-in flash on the IS-series cameras makes it simple to take correctly exposed flash photographs. In Program exposure mode, the camera will pick the settings to produce the best overall flash exposure. The same is true for all of the subject-specific programs. However, there may be times when this is not what you want.

In Aperture Priority Mode, the camera will automatically select a shutter speed of 1/100 second for proper flash synchronization. You choose the aperture appropriate to the effect you want to create and the camera will balance the flash output to this aperture. Just remember, the smaller the aperture (or the higher the

For a pleasing portrait, there should be separation between the subject and background. Choosing a smaller aperture and keeping enough distance between the girl and her surroundings kept everything behind her from being illuminated by the flash. Photo: Günter Richter ➪

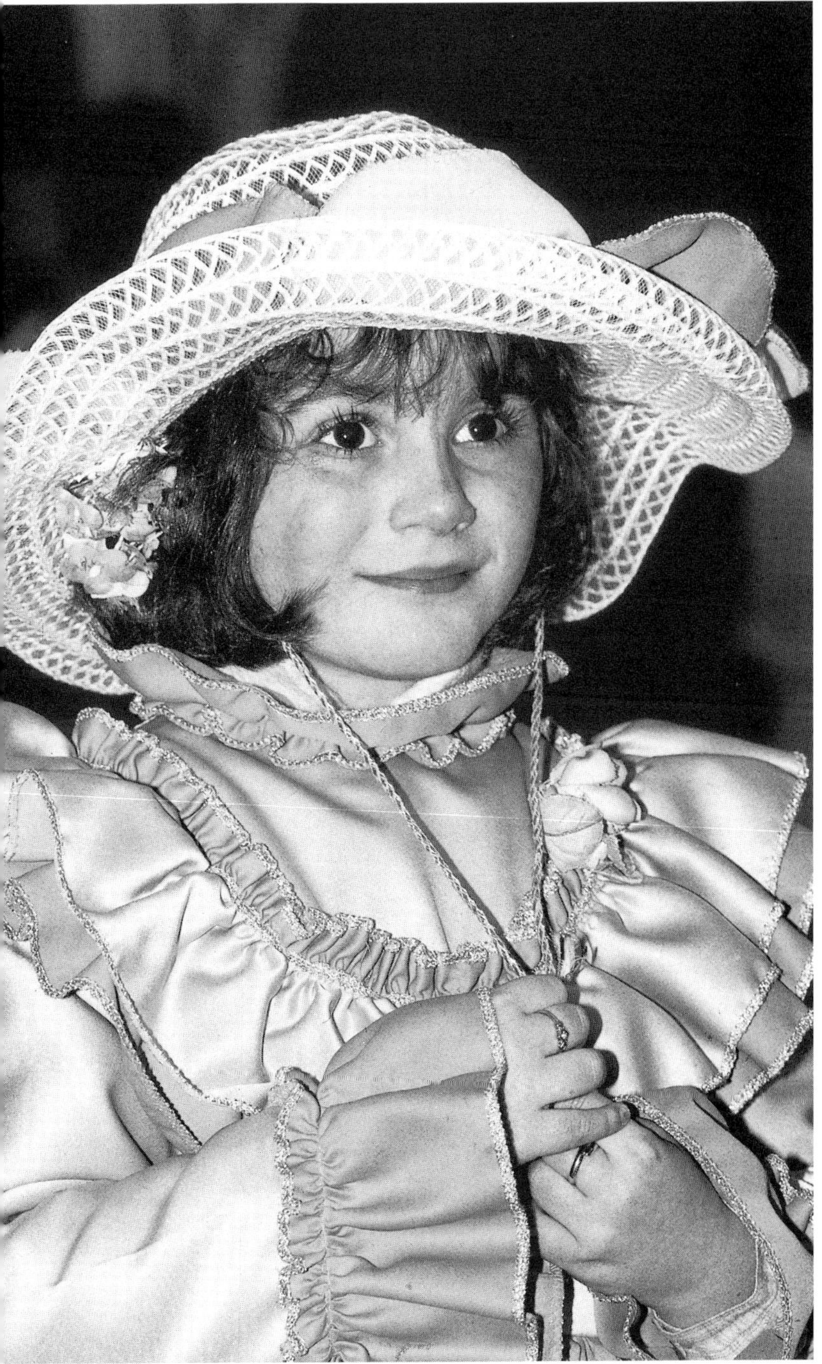

f/number), the less distance the flash will cover. This is useful for preventing the flash from illuminating the background, ensuring separation between the subject and its surroundings. Just be certain the subject is not too far from the camera for adequate exposure.

The advantage of using Shutter Priority mode with flash, is that you can choose slower shutter speeds to combine flash and ambient light. This is similar to what the camera does automatically using Night Scene program. In Shutter Priority and Manual modes, you must be careful not to set the shutter speed faster than 1/100 second for proper flash synchronization. At speeds faster than 1/100 second, the camera will allow the shutter release to be triggered, but the flash will not fire.

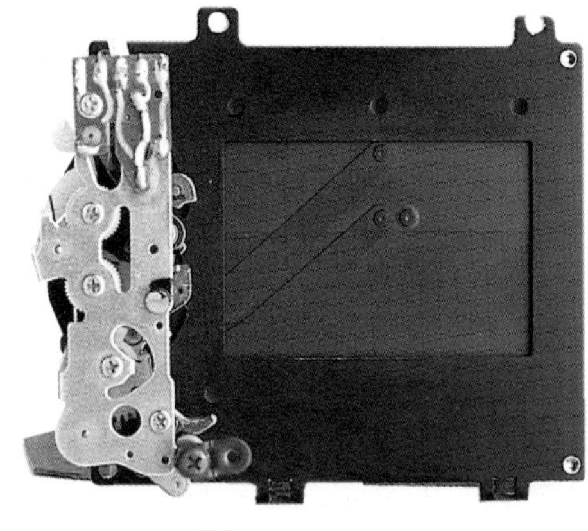

The focal plane shutter of the IS-series cameras is actually two multi-bladed shutter curtains. The first curtain is shown here covering the film window to prevent the film from being exposed.

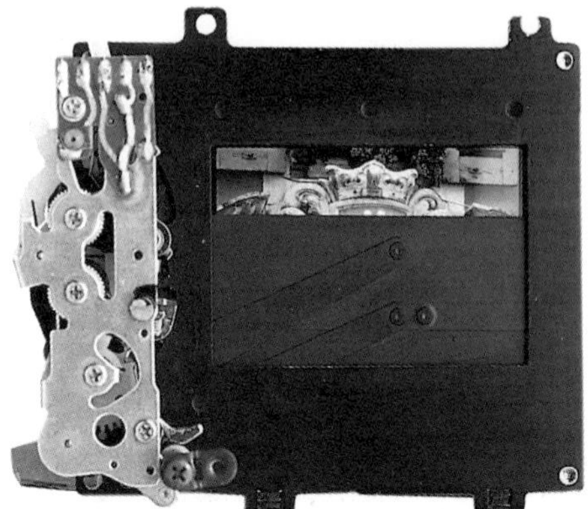

When the shutter release is pressed, the first curtain begins to open.

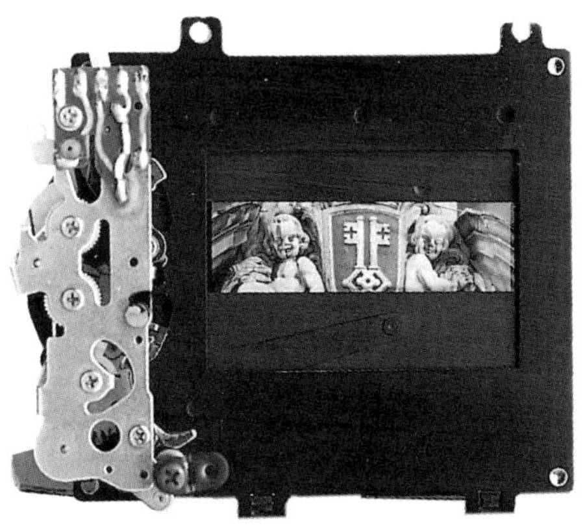

If a shutter speed faster than 1/100 second is set, the second curtain will begin to close before the first curtain has fully opened. This is not a problem with ambient light exposures, but the flash cannot be used at speeds faster than 1/100 second as only a portion of the film would be exposed.

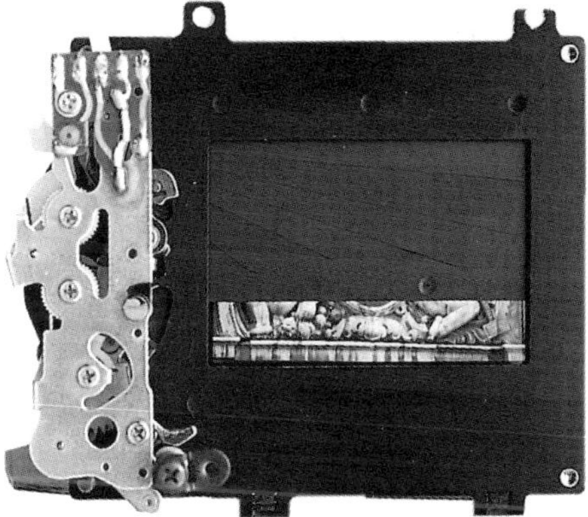

The second curtain comes down to cover the film and the camera automatically resets the shutter curtains to be in position for the next exposure.

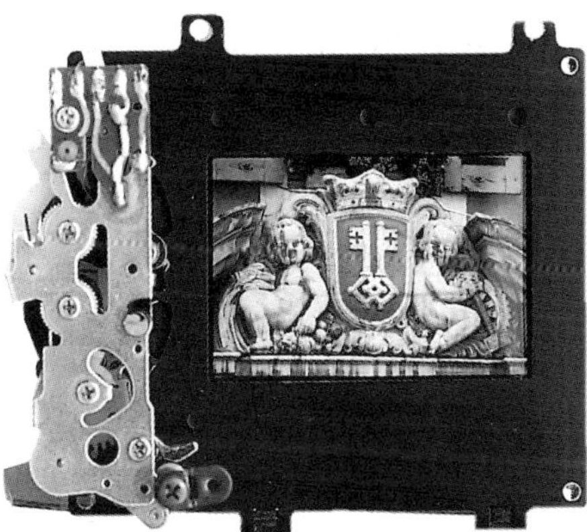

A shutter speed of 1/100 second or slower allows enough time for the first curtain to fully open before the second curtain begins to close. This is essential when using flash.

Flash synchronization: The camera's shutter actually consists of two curtains. The first curtain opens to expose the film and the second curtain follows to cover the film. Changing shutter speeds does not change how fast the shutter curtains move, only the length of time before the second shutter curtain covers the film. In flash photography, the flash must fire when the first curtain is completely open and before the second curtain begins to close. This determines the camera's flash synchronization speed; 1/100 second for the IS-series cameras.

Auto-S Mode

The IS cameras offer what Olympus calls Auto-S flash photography with their built-in flash units. This is a system to reduce the red-eye phenomenon. Red-eye is caused by light from the flash reflecting from the retina inside the subject's eye because their pupil is dilated and the flash axis is close to the lens axis. To help reduce this, select the Auto-S flash mode. When this mode is used the flash will emit a rapid succession of pre-flashes just before the picture is taken which will cause your subject's pupils to contract, minimizing red-eye. To set Auto-S mode, hold the flash button and scroll through the flash mode options until Auto-S is displayed on the LCD panel. Auto-S mode can be used with all exposure mode options except Manual mode.

Fill Flash

Because of the difficulty of use with older systems, I was not much of a fan of fill flash in the past. Either the flash was too bright and gave a very artificial look to the pictures or it was too dim and did not sufficiently reduce contrast in the picture. I approached claims from Olympus that the G40 and the built-in flash on the IS cameras would automate the process with skepticism. I must say that I was wrong to have doubted them. In all but a few situations, the Olympus flash has provided a perfect balance between ambient and flash lighting for fill flash photos that neither look artificial nor lack the necessary softening of contrast. I have shot hundreds of photos with the IS cameras using fill flash outdoors in daylight and find myself liking this system more with each session.

The camera can only be set for fill flash in the Program mode. This works well for general photography, providing just the right

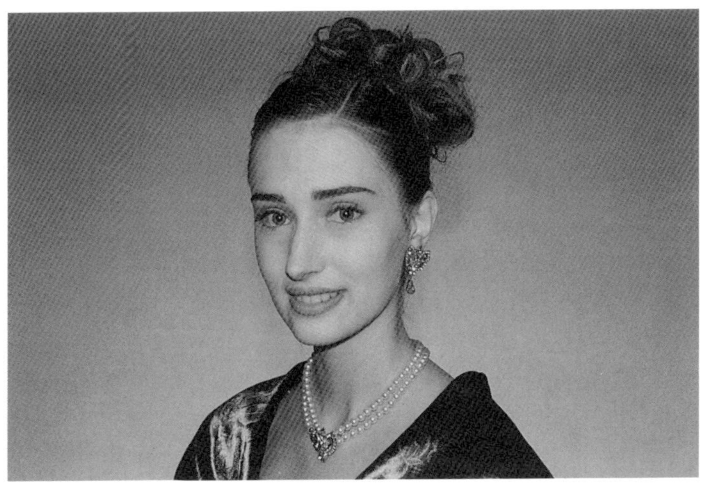

Above: When subjects are close, the built-in, variable-power flash unit automatically provides "soft flash" for more pleasing skin tones and softer shadows.

Below: When photographed with conventional flash, the same subject is overexposed and appears washed out.

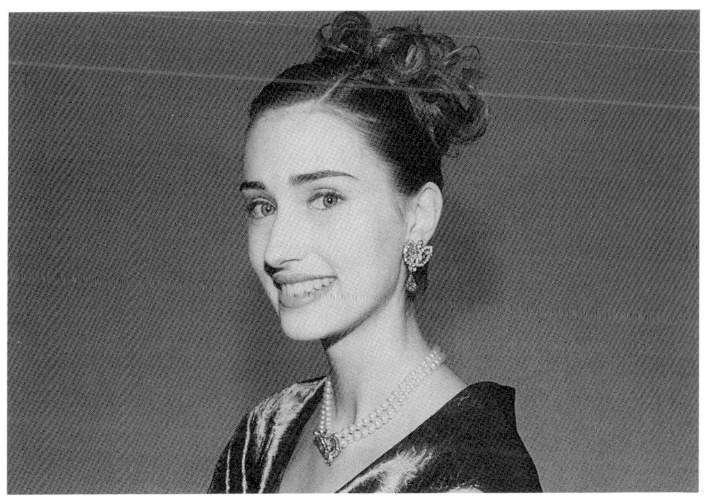

"kick" of fill flash to get rid of overly dark shadows without washing out the bright areas. Using fill flash in bright ambient light with rapidly moving subjects, however, may cause ghosting. This is a secondary image which is not aligned with the flash image or is streaked or blurred.

Bounce Flash

The flash head of the G40 flash is made so that it can be tilted. In its normal position, it is aligned with the axis of the lens, which is the best position for most fill flash photography. However, when taking photos in low ambient light or using the manual flash mode, having the flash head in this position may produce harsh shadows behind your subjects. To avoid or soften these shadows, a technique called bounce flash is used.

By tilting the head of the G40 flash upward, the light from the flash will reflect off the ceiling and illuminate your subject from above. This is perceived as more natural. Light bounced off the ceiling will also be softened so that the shadows will not be so harsh. To successfully illuminate a subject with bounced light, aim the flash to hit a point on the ceiling approximately halfway between you and .

It is important to keep in mind that this will only work well with a white ceiling which is not too high. Ceilings at about the usual eight foot height will work well, but a very high ceiling will not because the light must travel too far. In working with the flash directed at the subject, the light is simply traveling in a straight line from the flash to the subject. With bounce flash, you must figure the total distance the light travels from the flash to the ceiling and then to the subject. If a ceiling is too high, it may exceed the maximum distance the flash can cover. Also, it is important to use this technique only with white or neutral-colored ceilings if using color film, otherwise the light will take on the color of the ceiling and tint the entire photograph with it.

In addition to tilting, the head of the G40 flash also can be turned to the side. This can be used to bounce light off a nearby wall or flat surface if no ceiling is available, and allows light to be bounced off the ceiling with the camera turned for vertical photos. Bounce flash may be used in all the same modes as regular flash so long as you remember that the distance the light travels must not exceed the limits of the flash.

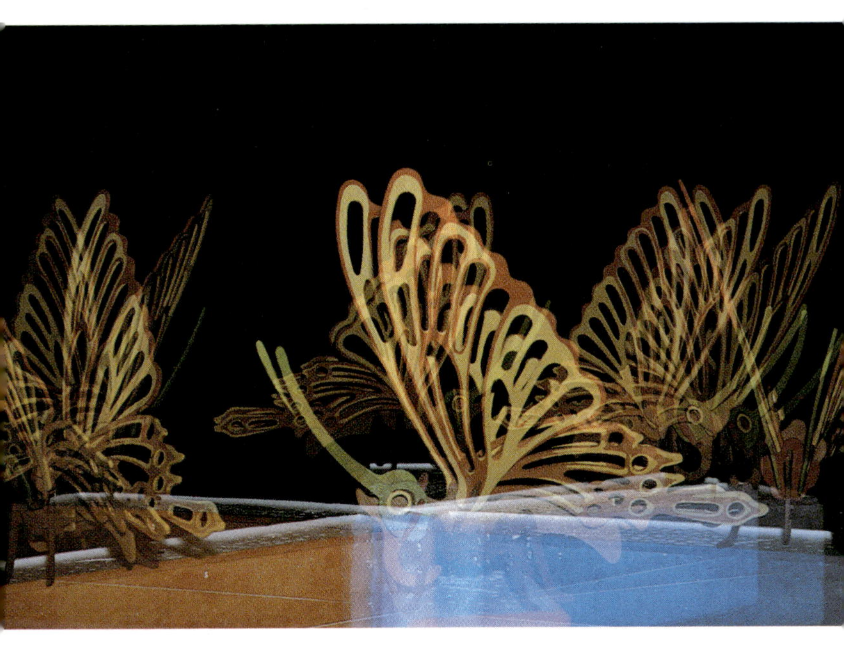

More interesting effects with your IS camera; this photograph was created using a G40 flash unit and a turntable. The prop was placed on the turntable and a slow shutter speed was set on the camera. The room was darkened and as the prop spun on the turntable, the flash was fired at regular intervals.

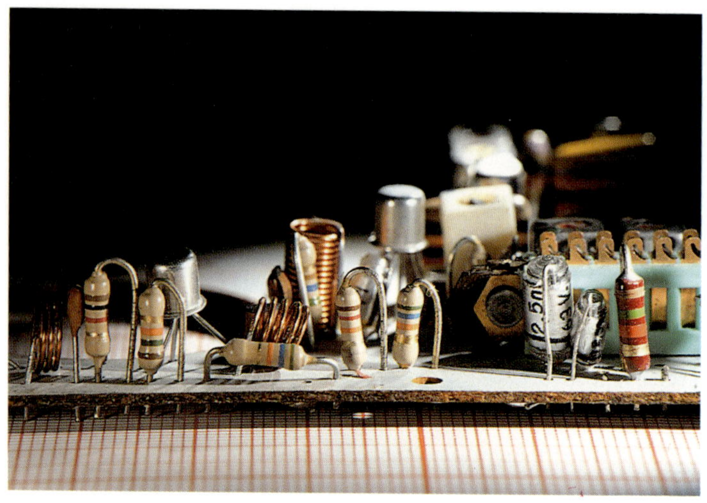

In Macro mode, the IS-3 can achieve a reproduction ratio of 1:5.

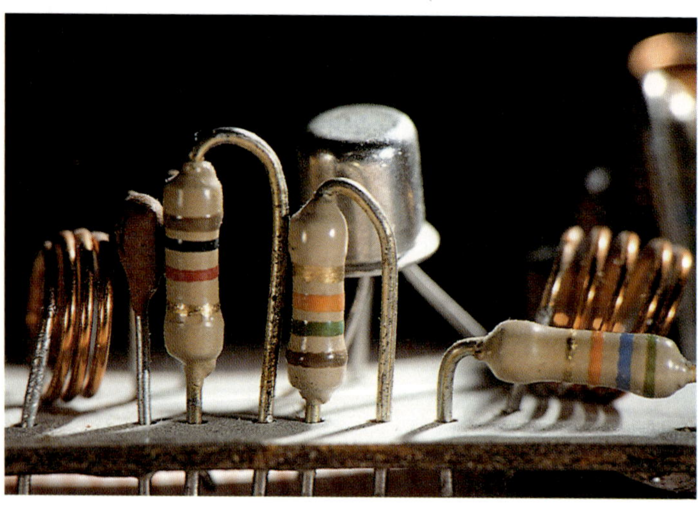

With the Macro Converter Lens, a reproduction ratio of 1:2 is possible.

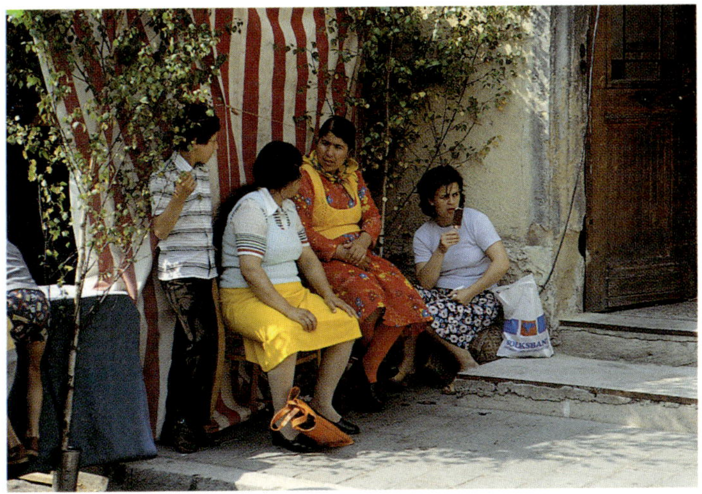

To capture subjects acting naturally, use a telephoto focal length setting and stand back. You're less likely to be noticed and the resulting photographs will not look posed.

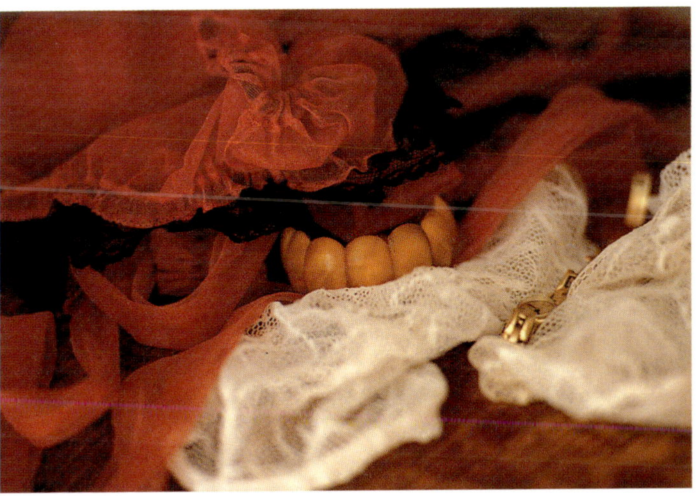

Diffused morning light and 1/3 stop underexposure made the colors in this still life look rich and warm, not washed out.

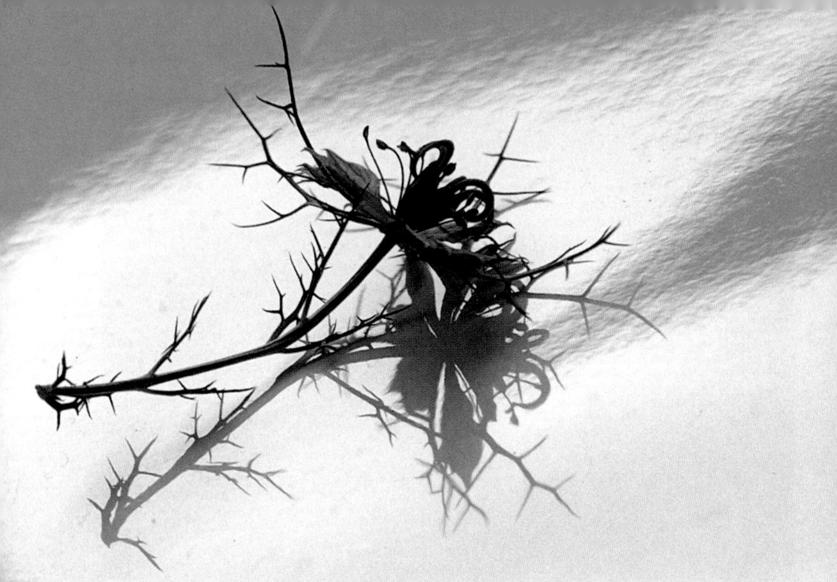

Exposure compensation was needed to prevent the reflective foil background from fooling the camera's meter. Setting the camera to overexpose the image kept detail in both the background and the flower.

Photo on page 114:
After a thunderstorm, the sky was an intense shade of blue, and the orange flowers stood out like a beacon. Spot metering was used to determine correct exposure for the flowers, and not the bright sky in the background.

High on a house, the photographer spotted this unique statue and used a focal length of 180mm to show it in detail. Aperture Priority mode was used and a small aperture was chosen for depth of field. The camera was set on a tripod because the lighting did not allow a fast enough shutter speed for handholding.

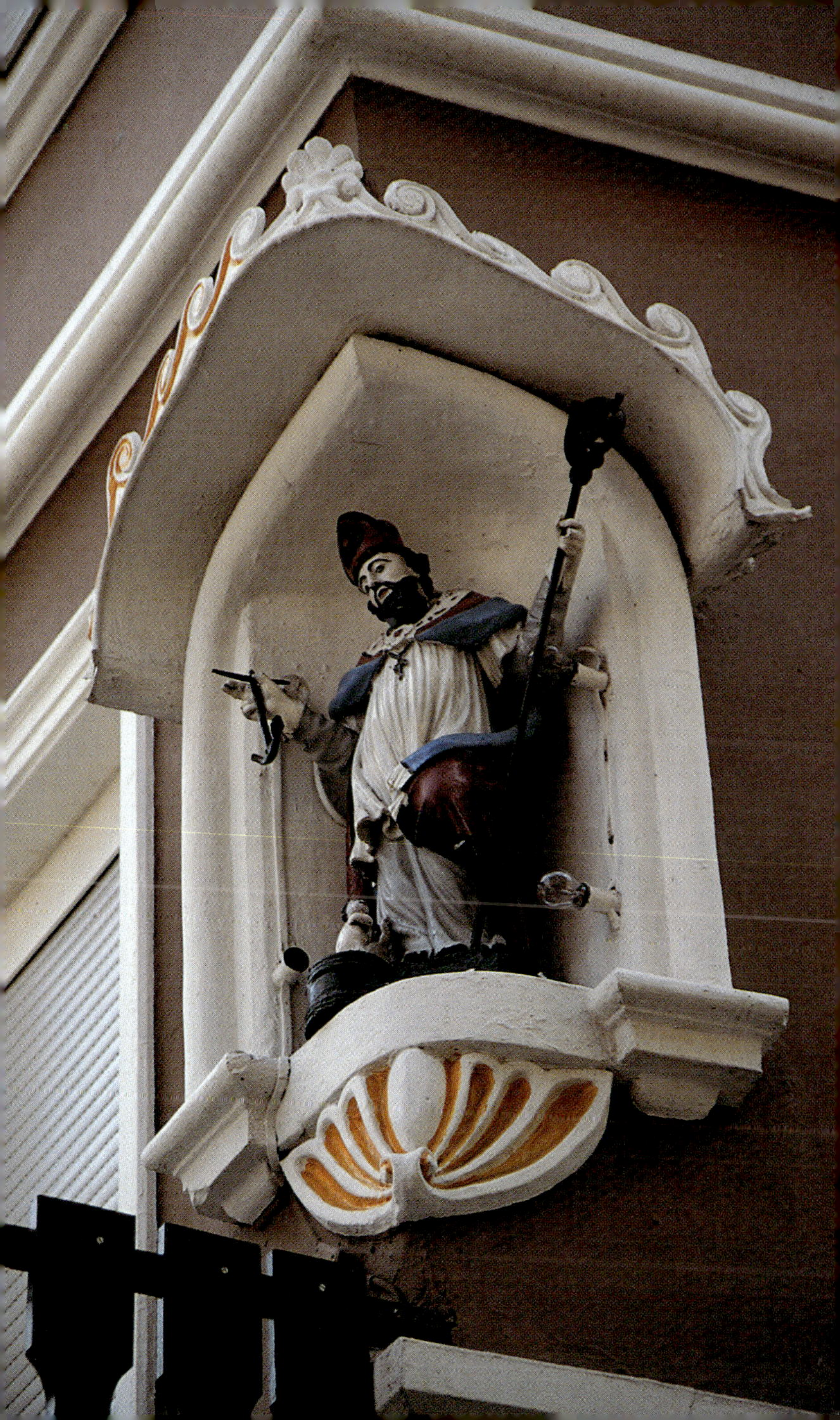

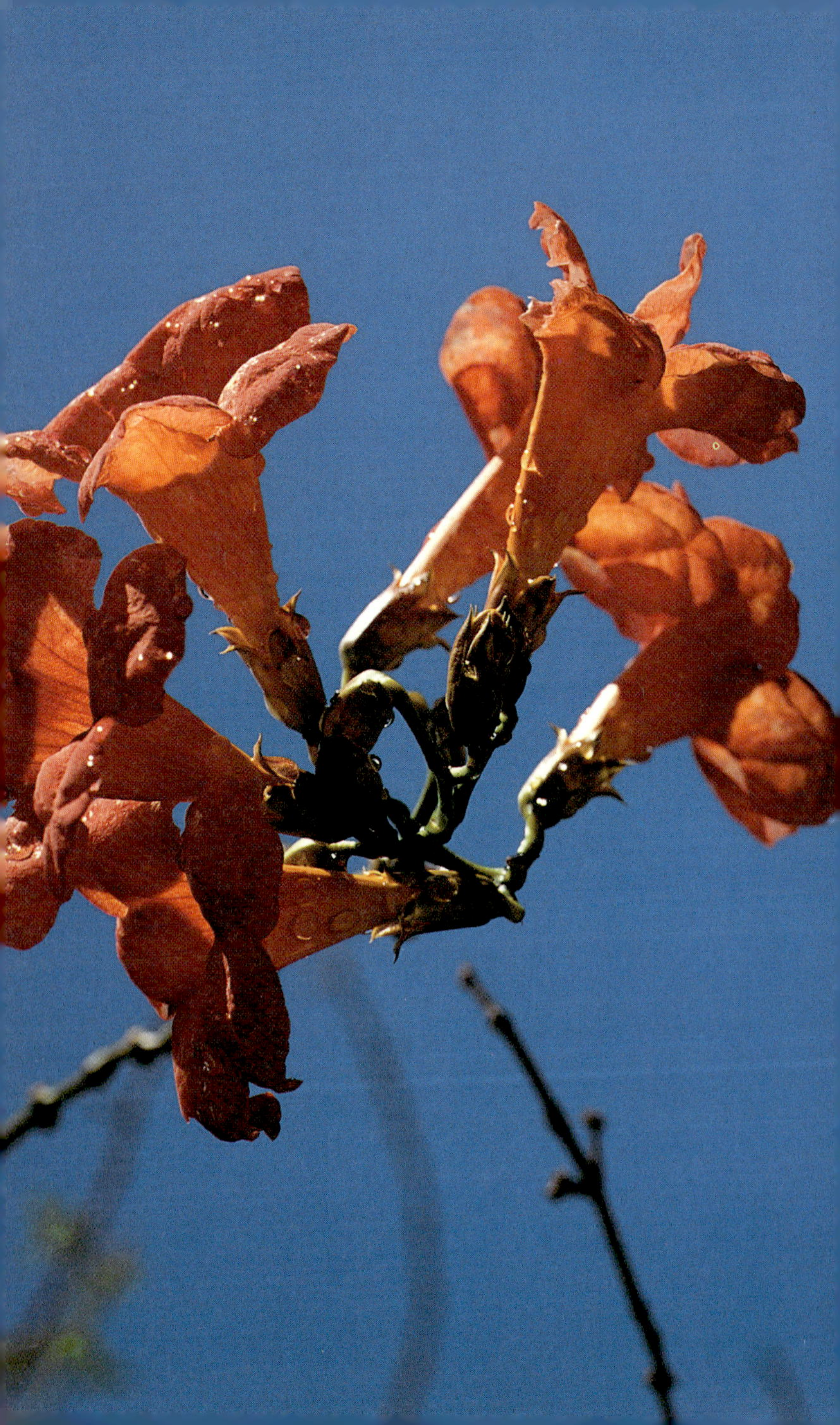

The camera's built-in flash exposed the photograph properly, but the lighting is not the most attractive for the subject. The position of the flash produced flat lighting and made the statue look two-dimensional. The direct light also caused sharp shadows along the edge of the statue and reflections on the shiny material used as a background.

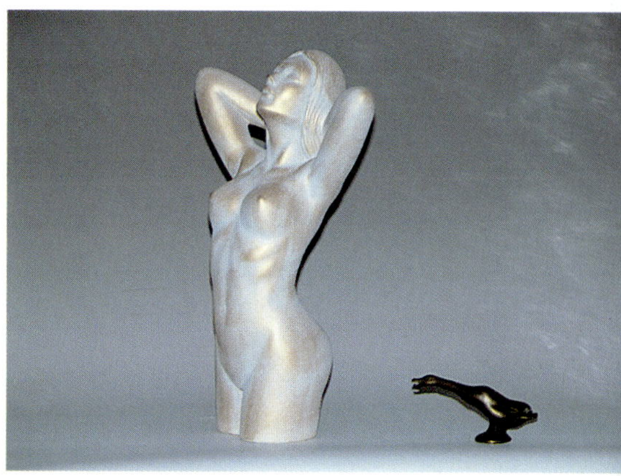

An accessory flash unit was connected to the camera with a dedicated cord and positioned to the left of the camera at a 45 degree angle. Side lighting emphasized surface detail on the statue, but harsh shadows and distracting highlights are still obvious because the flash is pointed directly at the subject.

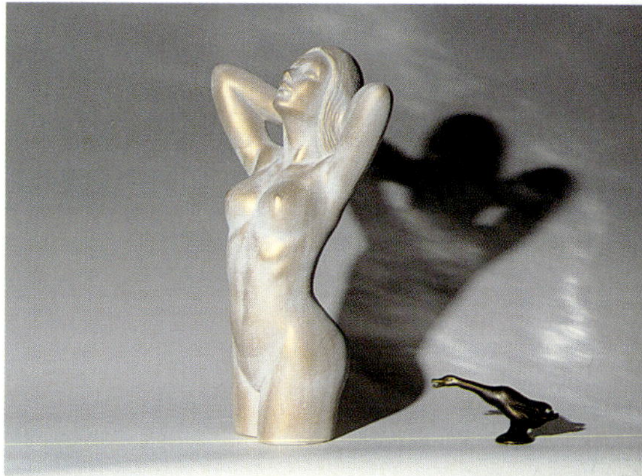

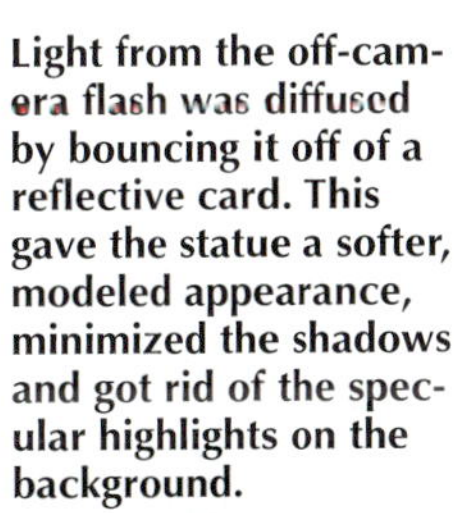

Light from the off-camera flash was diffused by bouncing it off of a reflective card. This gave the statue a softer, modeled appearance, minimized the shadows and got rid of the specular highlights on the background.

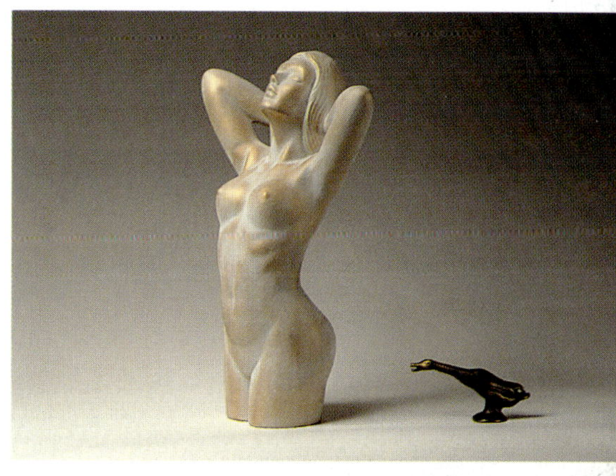

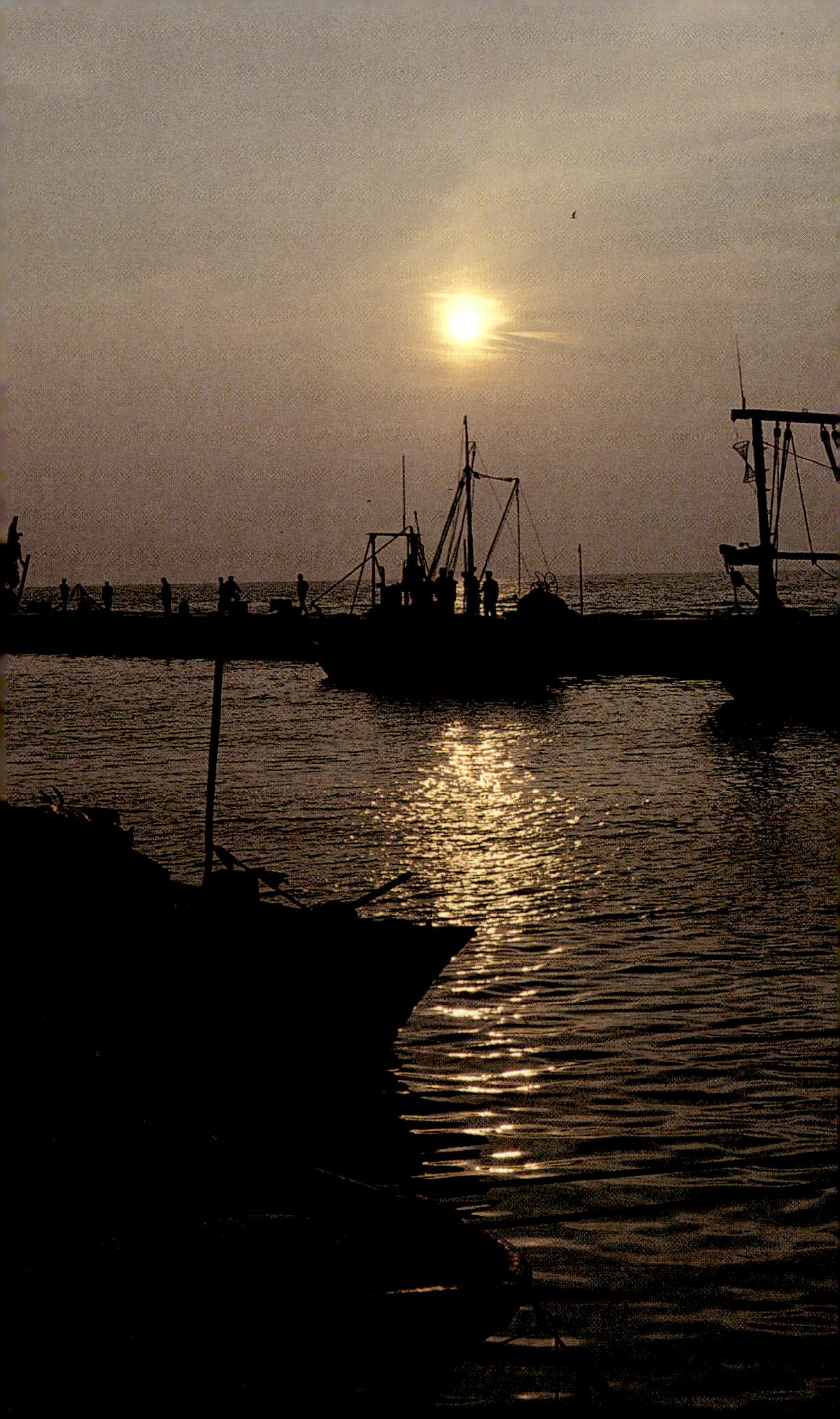

As an alternative to bouncing the light off a ceiling, some photographers point the flash head straight up and tape a white card behind it. The card is attached at an angle of about 45 to 90 degrees so that the light bounces off it and onto the subject. When photographed by light bounced from the ceiling, the subject may lack contrast and need just a little bit of direct flash to solve the problem. In this case a small white or silver card is taped to the flash head so that it throws just a little of the light more directly toward the subject. Such a card is called a "kicker". Many photographers create one of these in a pinch from a business card.

The G40 flash is also equipped with a pre-flash system to assist the camera's autofocus system in dim light. This pre-flash sends a burst of red light toward the subject when the shutter release button is pressed halfway. The beam is projected from the red colored area in the base of the flash just above the mounting shoe, and it is important when using the flash in dim light that you remember not to block this area.

Follow-Synchro Mode

The last capability of the G40 flash is Follow-Synchro mode, also called second curtain synchronization. When the G40 flash is set for this function, it will fire just before the second shutter curtain closes instead of just after the first curtain opens as in normal operation. In the case of long exposures, this allows the creation of photographs in which streaking can be used creatively to lead up to the image frozen by the flash. This is a somewhat unusual capability to have in a flash and you will have to learn by experimentation just what it can do for you.

⇦ **The photographer had to chose which part of this photograph was more important. If the men in the boat were exposed correctly to have visible detail, the sky would have been overexposed and the beautiful colors washed out. Instead, the exposure determination was based on the sky, and the boat and men became a silhouette.**

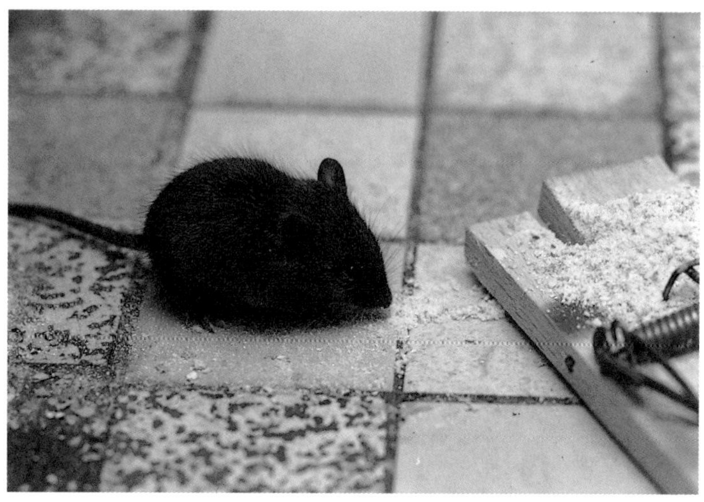

To get this photograph, the camera was set up in Program mode and bait was set out. When the mouse came along, the RC-100 Remote Control was used to trigger the camera from a distance.

Fast Flash Sync

(IS-3000 only, not on IS-3)

This feature allows you to use flash or fill flash at any shutter speed up to 1/2000 second. Unfortunately, due to patent licensing difficulties, this feature is not found on North American IS cameras. In operation, this system works by pulsing the flash rapidly at shutter speeds faster than 1/100, of a second producing the appearance of flash synchronization at speeds faster than the true maximum sync speed.

This system allows some types of photography which would be impossible otherwise, but with very limited flash power in this mode. Even with ISO 400 film your maximum shooting distance is only around ten feet.

Accessories

Because the Olympus IS cameras are self-contained photographic systems, few accessories are offered or needed.

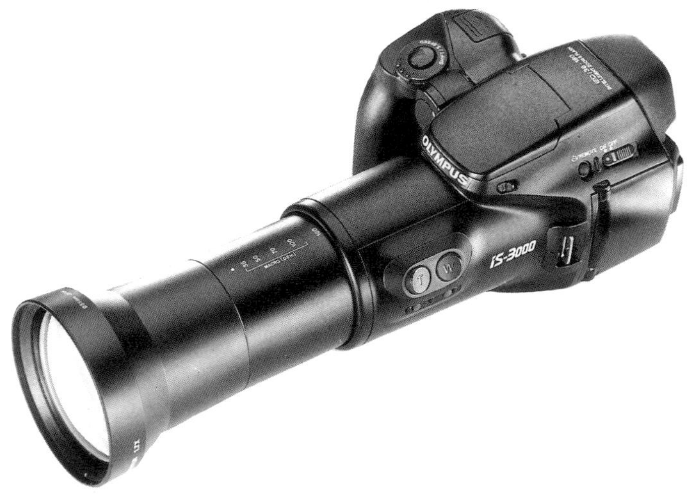

The IS-3 camera with the IS/L B-300 teleconverter lens.

PC Adaptor

One related point is that the Olympus IS cameras, although fully capable of producing professional results, lack the PC socket to allow them to be used with professional studio type flash units, or units from other manufacturers. This is due to the complex electronic routing system used to determine exposure. All is not lost, however, since Olympus does make a Multi-Synchro adapter which fits the IS-1, IS-2 and IS-3 cameras, and has a standard PC socket on top. This adapter is expensive, and big and bulky, but it does have the unique feature of allowing any flash to be used with the IS camera's second curtain sync capability.

Remote Control

There is also an optional Olympus RC-100 Remote Control which uses an infrared beam to fire the camera. It is compatible with the IS-3 and IS-10 cameras only. To use it, the camera must be set to recognize the infrared signal. This is done using the same button that sets the self-timer. The camera can be set to give a three second delay or on the IS-3 only, to fire the instant the remote is triggered. Use the RC-100 in place of a cable release for group shots, self-portraits or to lock open the shutter for vibration-free time exposures.

For the IS-2, 4 foot and 16 foot remote shutter release cords are available. These allow the shutter to be triggered remotely by the photographer.

Conversion Lenses

Olympus offers a series of lens converters which extend the range of coverage of the zoom lenses. The 35mm minimum focal length of the IS-2 and IS-3 cameras becomes 28mm. This is useful for those subjects for which 35mm simply isn't wide enough. There is no wide angle converter for the IS-10 since the zoom lens range is from 28 to 110mm.

Olympus also offers teleconverters specific to each camera model. The 135mm maximum focal length of the IS-1 and IS-2 is extended to 200mm, the 180mm long focal length of the IS-3 to 300mm and the 110mm long focal length of the IS-10 to 180mm. Olympus also offers the IS/L macro converters which screw into the front of the lens like a filter and allow you to focus on closer objects.

Diopter Eyepieces

The only other accessories offered or likely to be needed are several options on carrying cases and the variable diopter eyepiece adapter which allows you to dial in an eyesight correction factor from + 2 to - 4, for individual eyesight correction. This fits onto the camera eyepiece.

Photographs taken at various focal lengths - 28mm with the wide-angle conversion lens, 35mm, 80mm, and 135mm - illustrate the versatility of the IS-2's zoom lens. ➪

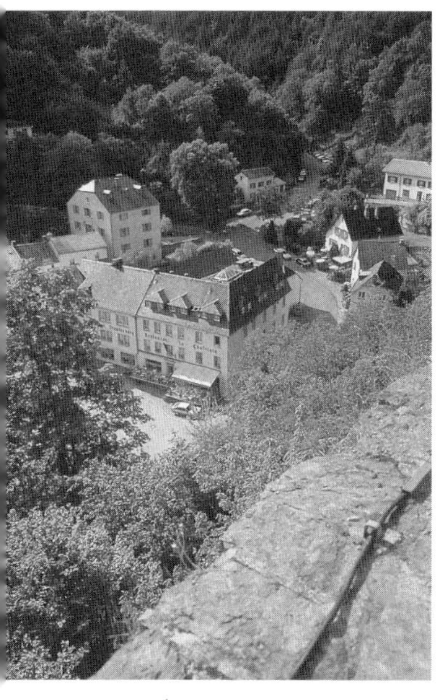

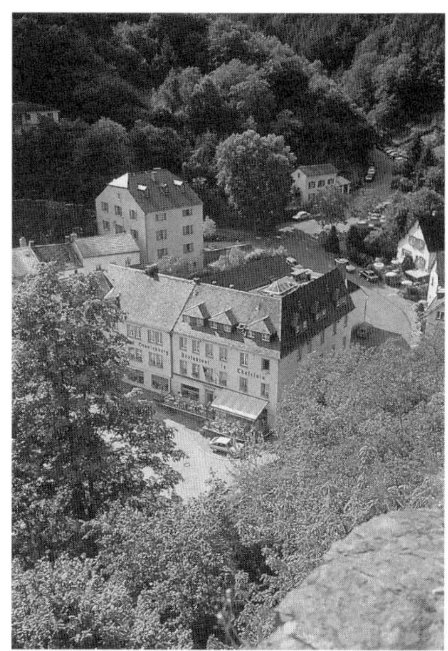

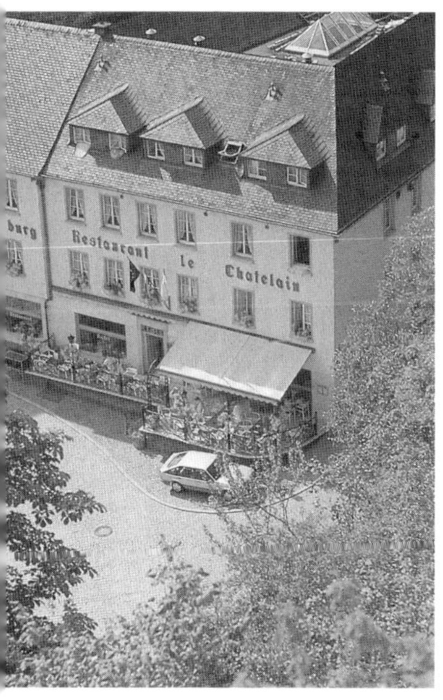
burg
Restaurant le Chatelain

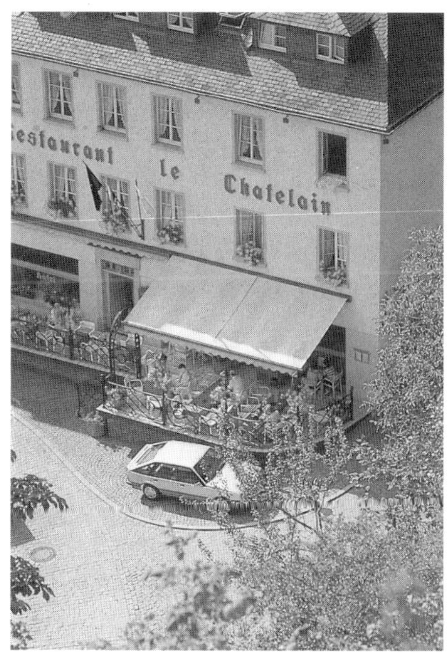
estaurant le Chatelain

Using the IS-2

The IS-2 is the second of Olympus' innovative SLR designs. It includes an integrated 35-135mm motorized zoom lens with ED glass. The cam-controlled automatic focus and s-shaped film path result in an exceptionally compact camera. The on-board flash unit features two flash tubes, and is distance and focal length-controlled. The film transport motor can be switched between single and continuous shooting.

Getting Started

The camera may be tested without sacrificing film. Without film the IS-2's electronic metering system is set on ISO 3200. If the camera's capabilities are to be tested at ISO 200, lightly press the +/- button beside the LCD panel with the left thumb and press the Shift button until 4.0 appears in the small frame next to +. This correction will be erased automatically as soon as the camera's back is opened. However, an attempt to trick the DX system with an empty film cartridge will result in an error function! (A film cartridge without a film leader is considered to be erroneously spooled film by the electronic system which switches off automatically! Obviously, the system does not know that this error was intentional in order to test the IS-2 in a cost-saving manner).

DX Coding

Five spring contacts in the cassette chamber read the checkerboard pattern on most film cassettes. This pattern, called the DX code, provides film speed information which is transferred in the form of an electrical signal to the IS-2's exposure meter. The DX code covers a film sensitivity range from ISO 25 to ISO 3200. If a film is used that has an ISO between the standard assigned values, the camera's meter will automatically be set to the next lower standard ISO value. Color negative films have enough latitude to cope easily with this slight overexposure.

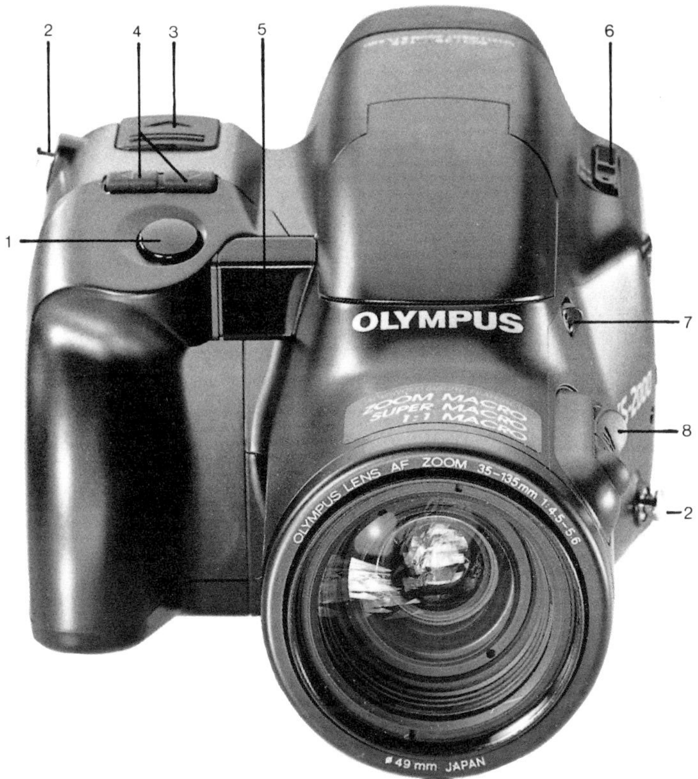

The Olympus IS-2:

1. Shutter release
2. Strap mounting lug
3. Flash shoe with cover
4. Shift buttons for shutter speeds, aperture values and correction factors
5. AF preflash window and self-timer release indicator
6. Power switch
7. Flash release
8. Zoom buttons

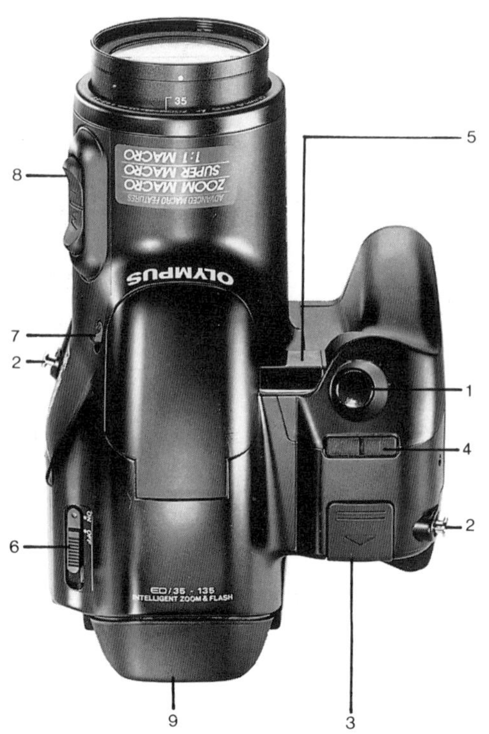

1. **Shutter release**
2. **Strap mounting lug**
3. **Flash shoe with cover**
4. **Shift buttons for shutter speeds, aperture values and correction factors**
5. **AF preflash window and self-timer release indicator**
6. **Power switch**
7. **Flash release**
8. **Zoom buttons**
9. **Viewfinder eyecup**

The IS-2 is always set to ISO 32 when a film cassette without a DX code is used. By pressing the +/- button in conjunction with the pair of buttons in front of the shutter release the IS-2 can be set for the correct ISO. A non-DX coded film up to ISO 200 can be used by applying the appropriate exposure compensation.

As mentioned above, the IS-2 will read the assigned ISO values directly off the DX code on the film cassette. By activating the buttons listed above, you may enter intermediate values into the program if you wish.

When no film is in the camera, the meter assumes an ISO of 3200. Exposure readings may seem unusually high until a film cassette is loaded.

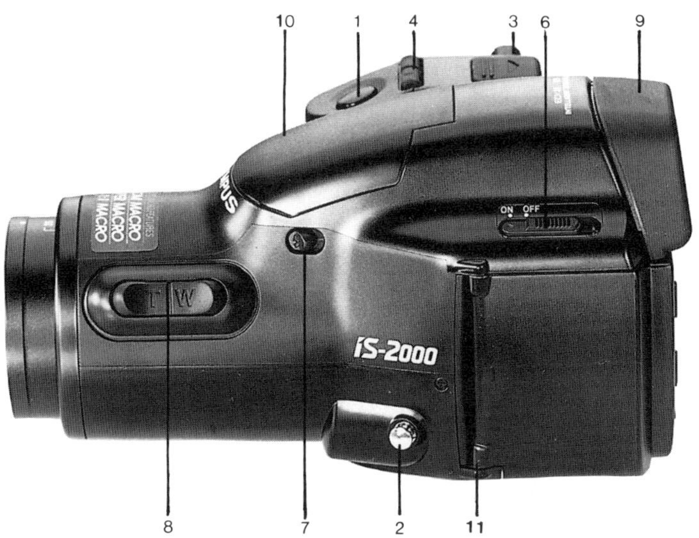

1. **Shutter release**
2. **Strap lug**
3. **Flash shoe with cover**
4. **Shift buttons for shutter speeds, aperture values and correction factors**
6. **Power switch**
7. **Flash release**
8. **Zoom buttons**
9. **Viewfinder eyecup**
10. **Flash**
11. **Camera back hinge**

Removing and Reloading Film

As soon as you have shot the last frame the IS-2 will immediately rewind the film. This is because a safety clutch stops the film advance whenever the film cassette no longer puts out any film

Occasionally photographers wish to rewind a partially exposed roll of film, usually to replace it with a different type or ISO. To accomplish this, the IS-2 has a tiny REWIND button which is best activated with the tip of a ballpoint pen. Professional laboratories do not require that the film leader project from the cassette. However, you will need it out if you wish to reload the partially exposed film back into the IS-2. Film leader retrievers are available at most camera stores.

To reload a partially exposed film, switch on your IS-2, activate the FUNCTION and MODE keys to cause M to blink and then

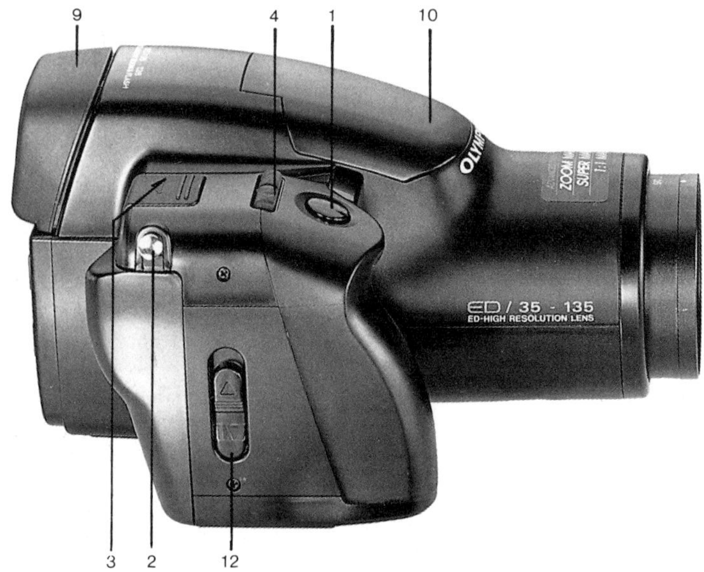

The IS-2's prominent handgrip on the right side makes holding the camera very comfortable.

1. **Shutter release**
2. **Strap lug**
3. **Flash shoe with cover**
4. **Shift buttons for shutter speeds, aperture values and correction factors**

9. **Viewfinder eyecup**
10. **Flash**
12. **Camera back release**

press the FUNCTION button again in order to input the manual settings of shutter speed and aperture. Then, activating the right button in front of the shutter release, reduce the aperture to its smallest setting. Holding down the +/- button, use the same button to set the shutter to 1/2000 sec. and put the lens cap on the lens. Briefly tap the PF button, and the autofocus function will be disabled. Now the IS-2 is ready for reloading. When 1 is displayed on the LCD, press the release until the counter indicates the frame number at which you removed the film from the IS-2 (and, hopefully, noted on the cassette). Press the release again twice more to make certain there is no overlap of frames. Press the RESET button to "exit" this tricky mode and return to standard operation of the IS-2.

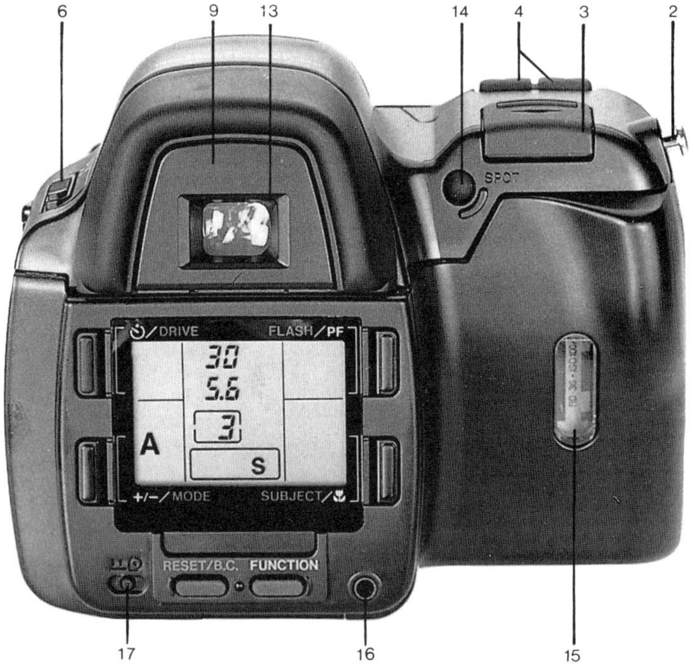

2. **Strap lug**
3. **Flash shoe with cover**
4. **Shift buttons for shutter speeds, aperture values and correction factors**
6. **Power switch**
9. **Viewfinder eyecup**
13. **Viewfinder**
14. **Spot metering button**
15. **Film cassette viewing window**
16. **Remote release socket**
17. **Rewind button** **(See also, illustration on page 128.)**

Film Advance

The film advance motor located in the rear of the camera receives commands in two ways:

One is by activating the RESET button which returns the IS-2 to single frame advance, automatic programming and multi-zone metering. The S (SINGLE) in the lower part of the LCD panel indicates that the IS-2 will take only one exposure when the release is pressed. The camera will not fire, however, until the autofocus mechanism has locked onto a point of focus.

The IS-2 Information System

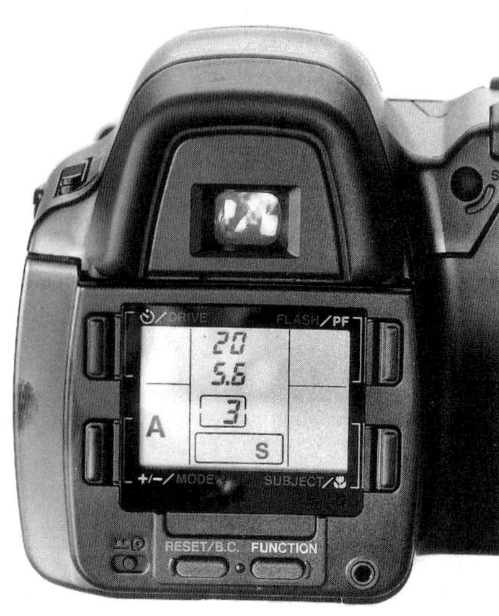

The rear of the IS-2 camera showing "Control Central." This includes the 36 x 24 mm LCD panel which provides information on just about any input data required. The Mode, Drive, Flash and Subject selection buttons are located around the LCD screen. Below this are the Function and Reset buttons.

FUNCTION: This button works in conjunction with the Mode, Drive, Flash and Subject buttons to access and set their primary functions. When the FUNCTION button is pressed lightly, all function symbols are displayed on the LCD panel; activated symbols blink. After selecting new functions by activating the appropriate keys, the FUNCTION button must be pressed again to enter the selection.

RESET: The quickest way to set the camera to fully-automatic control is by pressing the Reset button. It is also the battery check button.

MODE: Exposure modes are accessed on the IS-2 camera by pressing the Function button and then selecting various options with the Mode button (P, A, M). The function button is then depressed a second time to lock in the selected mode. The Mode button is used without the Function button to set exposure compensation.

DRIVE: When used with the Function button, the Drive button is used to select Single or Continuous film advance modes. Double exposure mode D.EXP is also available. This button is also used to set the self-timer.

PF/FLASH: Select Auto, Auto-S, or fill flash mode by first pressing the Function button Switches the AF motor directly from automatic to manual focus. Manual focus is adjusted using the zoom buttons.

By using the DRIVE button, located on the top to the left of the LCD, additional film transport modes can be selected. Once a mode is selected the FUNCTION button must be lightly depressed to enter the command. The DRIVE cycle consists of three transport modes, S - single frame advance, C - continuous advance, and D.EXP - double-exposure. You must follow this progression through the DRIVE cycle each time the DRIVE button is pressed. The selected transport mode is indicated by blinking characters on the LCD. Remember, the FUNCTION button must be pressed to enter the selected mode.

Continuous Film Advance

In the C mode, as long as the shutter release is pressed, the IS-2 will take a continuous sequence of shots at 2 frames per sec. The IS-2 will maintain this rate as long as the subject brightness and distance do not change during the half second between shots. This is because the camera's computer verifies these settings for each exposure. If nothing changes, nothing needs to be corrected and the camera is immediately enabled for the next shot. Occasionally, more time is required between shots for corrections as necessitated by significant subject changes. In these situations the shooting frequency may decrease to one frame per second or less. Also, even under the best of conditions, the IS-2 will maintain a rate of 2 frames per second only when the shutter speed is faster than 1/30 second.

Two frames per second or even 10 frames in 5 seconds is not sufficient to capture a rider leaning his motor-cycle through a hairpin curve. However, this shooting frequency is adequate for shooting a monkey swinging from branch to branch in an outdoor setting.

When the IS-2 is in continuous mode it offers an enticing way to capture the world passing by. However, do not forget that when you move to this one-half second beat, the last frame will be reached in only 22 seconds! While you try to change the film at record speed, the nicest scenes may be passing by. Frequently, several short sequences of fewer shots may provide better results than a lead finger on the release.

When using flash with the IS-2 in continuous mode, the electronic system will always adjust the shutter speed to 1/100 sec.

Depending on the subject and the shooting distance, the power stored by the flash capacitor may only be adequate for two shots in a series. When the capacitor has discharged, the shutter automatically switches to the speed required for the ambient light exposure. This speed may be too slow for sharp hand-held exposures.

If you want to return from C to S without using the RESET button, press the DRIVE button twice but do not forget to press the FUNCTION button to enter the change.

Program Auto Exposure

Automatic programming is achieved by two techniques:
The first is to lightly press the RESET button. This disables all previously set functions, programs and correction factors and switches the IS-2 to single-frame advance and multi-zone metering.

The second technique is to briefly press the FUNCTION button and hold down the MODE button until P begins to blink on the left edge of the LCD panel. The FUNCTION button must again be pressed lightly to enter the P command. This method retains all previously set special functions and correction factors.

The IS-2's LCD keeps you informed of all selections. This easy-to-read panel will display P for automatic programming, S for sin-

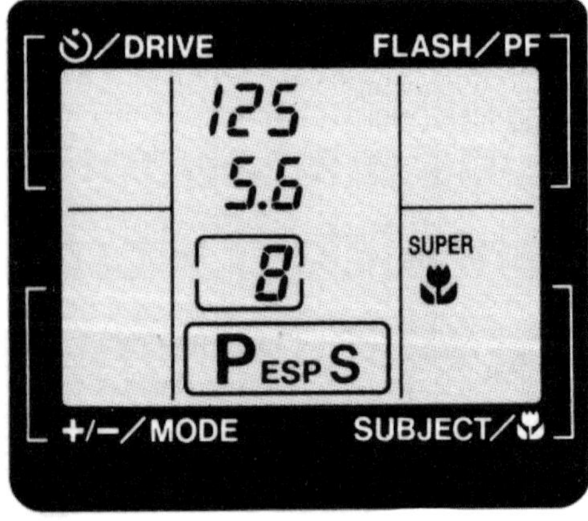

From top to bottom, the shutter speed is 1/125 second and the aperture is f/5.6. The roll of film is on its eighth exposure. P stands for Program exposure mode and ESP is the multi-zone exposure metering function. The selected Drive mode is single frame advance (S) and the Super Macro mode is engaged.

gle-frame advance and, in between, ESP for multi-zone metering (only in automatic programming mode) and the number of the next frame. To save power, the display disappears after 30 sec. A light press of the shutter release recalls this readout for another 30 sec. along with the shutter speed and aperture values determined by the automatic programming.

The fuzzy logic-based ESP multi-zone exposure metering feature evaluates exposure data based on light and dark subject areas. Automatic programming will only let you take a photograph if the subject is in focus.

You may put the IS-2 against your right or left eye, whichever you prefer. Then select the best composition with the zoom while placing the subject properly in the viewfinder rectangle. Then press the shutter release lightly. A buzzing sound for a fraction of a second indicates that the autofocus motor has focused the lens. At the very top on the right edge of the viewfinder the green "O.K." LED indicates that the lens has been focused correctly. The field beneath it remains blank when there is sufficient light for hand-held exposures in the normal range. The next two lines indicate the programmed shutter speed and aperture value (as on the LCD panel). Blinking displays relating to spot metering and exposure correction appear in the lower-most field displaying viewfinder information. These viewfinder displays disappear about 30 seconds after you take your finger off the release.

As long as the shutter release is pressed half way the zoom rocker switch remains disabled. There is a reason for this: As the focal length is changed from 35mm to 135mm the zoom lens aperture decreases from 1:4.5 to 1:5.6. As a result all the other aperture values are reduced by just about one third of an aperture value. Consequently, the camera must recompute the exposure each time the focal length is changed.

Warning Signals

If the green autofocus LED is blinking, this means that the AF system cannot find focus and the shutter release is locked. Thus, the IS-2 will not take an out of focus photo. If you wish to do this for creative reasons, you must switch to power (manual) focus.

If the flash symbol under the autofocus LED is blinking, the exposure control thinks that the subject is too dark and that the shutter speed is too slow for sharp hand-held shots. The camera is telling you that you need to use flash.

The Four Motor System

The IS-2 has four motors that operate the various features and functions. The camera's CPU controls their operation but so you can have a better understanding of how the camera works, we have included a brief description of their functions.

Motor 1 is designed for forward and reverse film transport.

Motor 2 resets the mirror and the shutter curtains to starting position and at the same time cocks their drive springs.

Motor 3 drives the zoom action of the lens.

Motor 4 is the autofocus motor which is activated when the shutter release is pressed lightly. This motor adjusts the lens to the shooting distance based on the part of the subject framed by the small rectangle in the center of the viewfinder.

Using the IS-3

Although in-camera film-advance motors are a high-tech convenience, their squeaking, humming, chirping and beeping can often be annoying. One advanced feature of the IS-3 is that it is one of the quietest SLR cameras available on the market today.

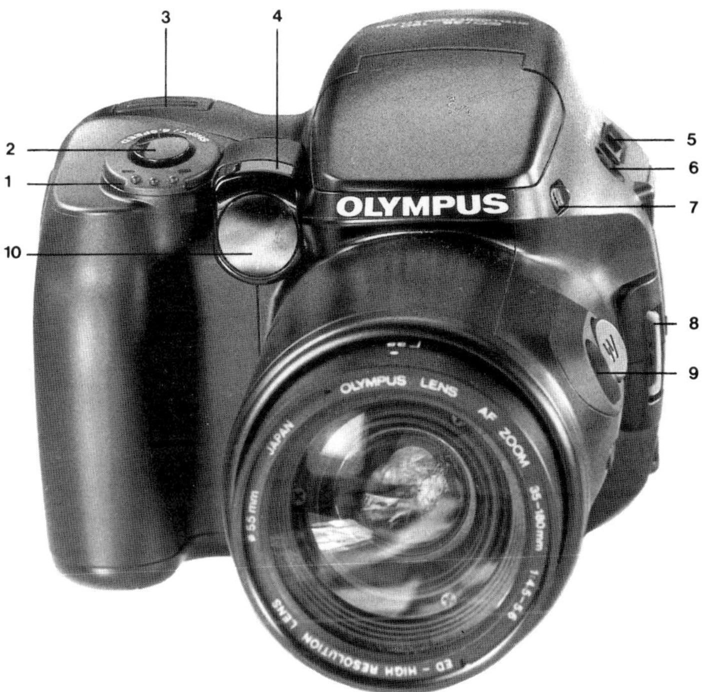

1. **Shift dial for shutter speeds, exposure control, special functions**
2. **Shutter release**
3. **Flash shoe with cover**
4. **Rear sensor for IR remote release**
5. **On/off switch**
6. **Switch for self-timer and IR remote release function**
7. **Flash release button**
8. **Strap lug**
9. **Zoom buttons**
10. **Illuminator for AF preflash, self-timer LED and sensor for IR remote release**

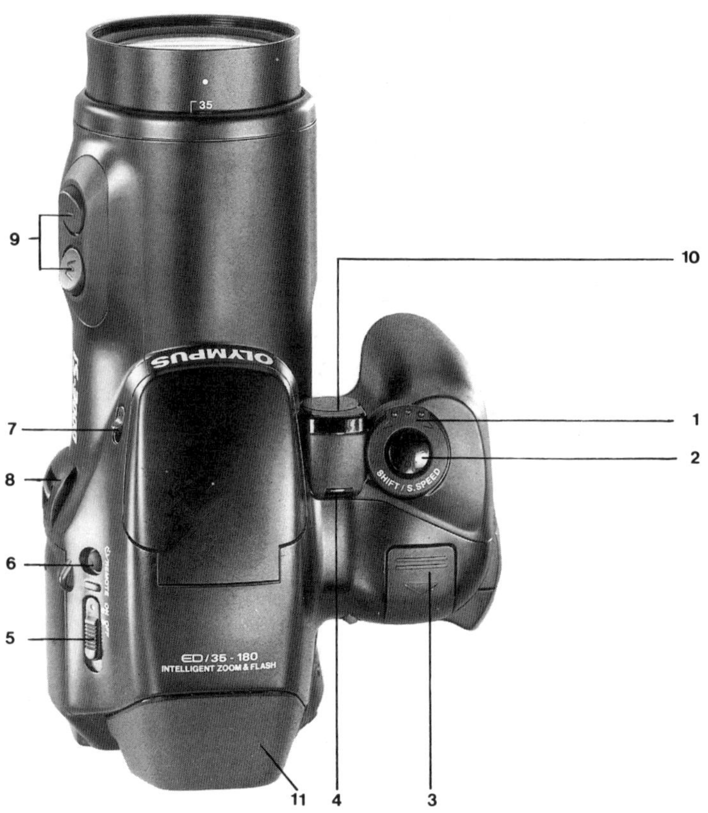

1. **Shift dial for shutter speeds, exposure control, special functions**
2. **Shutter release**
3. **Flash shoe with cover**
4. **Rear sensor for IR remote release**
5. **Power switch**
6. **Self-timer/Remote control button**
7. **Flash release**
8. **Strap lug**
9. **Zoom buttons**
10. **Illuminator for AF preflash, self-timer LED and sensor for IR remote release**
11. **Viewfinder eyecup**

Because of the expanded zoom capability offered by the IS-3, interchangeable lenses are no longer necessary. The IS-3's zoom lens covers focal lengths from 35 to 180mm. Plus, with wide-

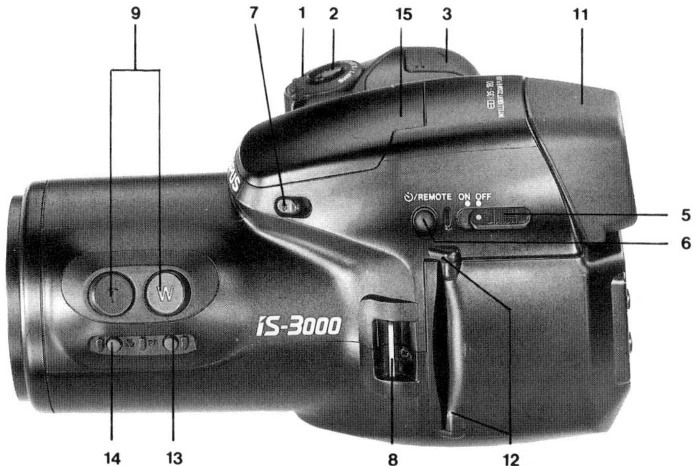

1. Shift dial for shutter speeds, exposure control, special functions
2. Shutter release
3. Flash shoe with cover
5. Power switch
6. Self-timer/Remote control button
7. Flash release
8. Strap lug
9. Zoom buttons
11. Viewfinder eyecup
12. Camera back hinges
13. PF button switches the AF motor to manual focus
14. Macro button
15. Flash

angle and telephoto attachments this may be extended to a range from 28 to 300mm. (There is no zooming, however, 180 to 300mm or 35 to 28mm.)

Consistent with Olympus-family tradition, the IS-3's state-of-the-art features include: a top-performance motorized 35-180mm zoom lens incorporating ED glass, automatic focus, S-wrap film guide, sleek camera body design, integrated twin-bulb flash unit controlled by distance and focal length, motorized film transport for individual and continuous exposures, and a low-profile SLR viewfinder.

For close-up shots, the B-MACRO accessory converter allows a reproduction ratio of 1:2. When high-speed films are used and the IS-3 is mounted to a tripod, the lower effective speed of the lens with the converter may be compensated for adequately.

A final feature of modern camera design is the integrated flash unit. Although light projected directly at the subject from an on-

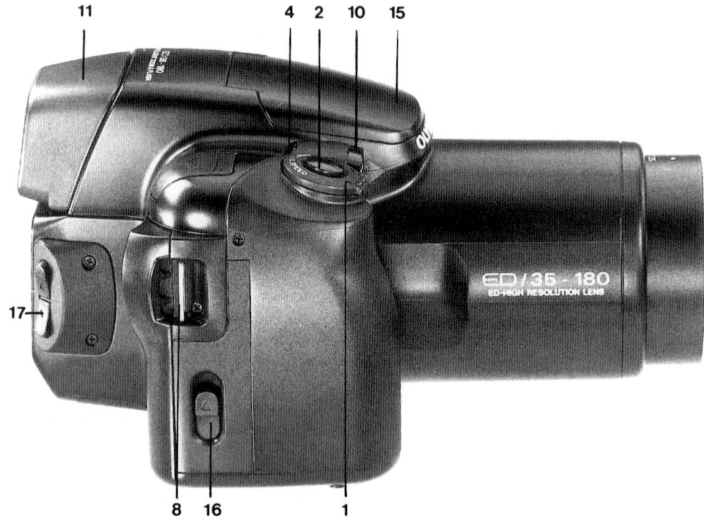

1. Shift dial for shutter speeds, exposure control, special functions
2. Shutter release
4. Rear sensor for IR remote release
8. Strap lug
10. Illuminator for AF preflash, self-timer LED and sensor for IR remote release
11. Viewfinder eyecup
15. Flash
16. Camera back release
17. Shift buttons for exposure control, special functions

camera flash may not be the most elegant form of illumination, this feature appears to enjoy increasing, acceptance due to its convenience.

Getting Started

The fuzzy logic-based ESP multi-zone exposure metering feature evaluates exposure data based on light and dark subject areas. Automatic programming will only let you take a photograph if the subject is in focus.

Look through the viewfinder of the IS-3 with your right or left eye, whichever you prefer. Then select the best composition with the zoom while placing the subject properly in the viewfinder rectangle. Press the shutter release lightly and a buzzing sound

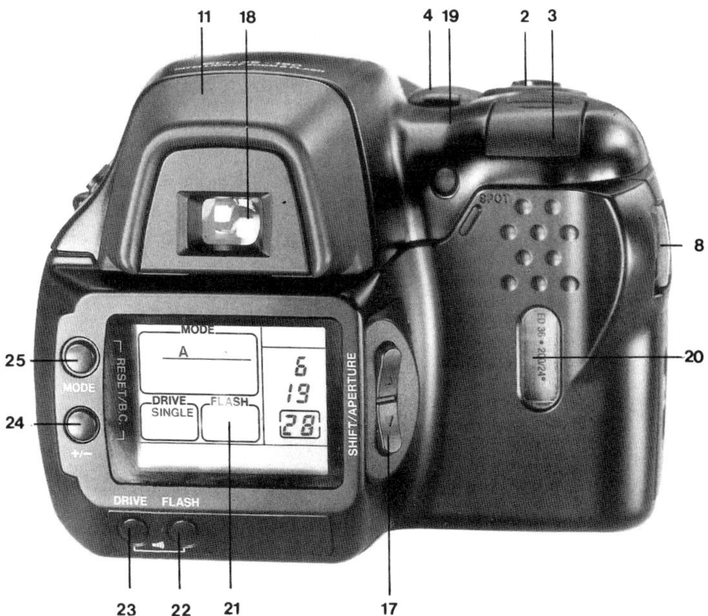

2. Shutter release
3. Flash shoe with cover
4. Rear sensor for IR remote release
8. Strap lug
11. Viewfinder eyecup
17. Shift buttons for exposure control, special functions
18. Viewfinder
19. Spot metering button
20. Film cassette viewing window
21. LCD panel
22. Flash mode button
23. Drive mode button (The two buttons above, together deactivate the beeper. It will be automatically reset when the camera is switched off and on again.)
24. Exposure compensation +/- button
25. MODE button for exposure options. (Both buttons make up the RESET function and battery test.)

indicates that the autofocus motor has focused the lens. At the very top on the right edge of the viewfinder the round green LED indicates that the lens has been focused correctly. The second field displays the lighting bolt to indicate flash is needed and the macro symbol if this mode is selected. The next two lines indicate the programmed shutter speed and aperture value and are the same as on the LCD panel. Blinking displays relating to spot

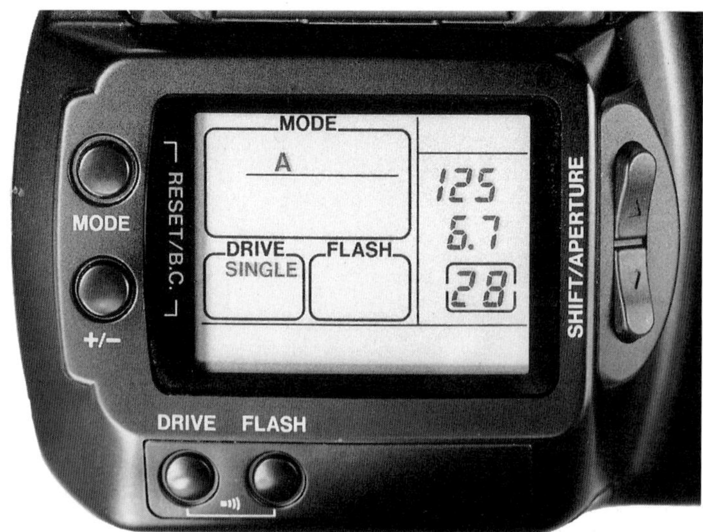

The LCD panel and main controls for the IS-3

The LCD panel on the IS-3 displays all camera control functions, except focusing information. Going clockwise around the LCD panel, the exposure mode setting is in the top left corner, indicated here as "A" or Aperture Priority. Along the right side, 125 means a shutter speed of 1/125 second is set, the aperture is 6.7 and the roll of film is on its 28th frame. Along the bottom, the flash has not been activated and the drive mode is single frame advance.

SHIFT/APERTURE: Controls the aperture setting in Aperture Priority and Manual mode. Can be used with the control buttons to scroll through and select various control functions.

MODE: Push the Mode button and use the Shift/Aperture button to scroll through the Exposure mode options. Release the Mode button to set the appropriate Exposure mode.

+/- : Sets exposure compensation. When used with the Mode button, the two buttons are a battery check and with the Shift/Aperture button, can instantly reset the camera to fully automatic operation.

DRIVE: Use this button in the same manner as described for the Mode button to set the Film Advance mode.

FLASH: When the flash is activated, the Flash button is used in conjunction with the Shift/Aperture button to select a Flash mode. If Drive and Flash are pushed simultaneously, they engage and disengage the audible autofocus signal.

metering and exposure correction appear in the lower-most field displaying viewfinder information. These viewfinder displays disappear about 30 seconds after you take your finger off the release.

As long as the shutter release is pressed half way the zoom rocker switch remains disabled. There is a reason for this: As the focal length is changed from 35mm to 180mm, the zoom lens aperture decreases from 1:4.5 to 1:5.6. As a result all the other aperture values are reduced by just about one third of an aperture value. Consequently, the camera must recompute the exposure each time the focal length is changed.

DX Coding

Five spring contacts in the cassette chamber read the checkerboard pattern on most film cassettes. This pattern, called the DX code, provides film speed information which is transferred in the form of an electrical signal to the IS-3's exposure meter. The DX code covers a film sensitivity range from ISO 25 to ISO 5000 in 1/3 stop increments. Non-DX coded film will be set to ISO 32. With no film in the camera, the IS-3 assumes an ISO of 3200.

Removing and Reloading Film

As soon as you have shot the last frame, the IS-3 will immediately rewind the film. This is because a safety clutch stops the film advance whenever the film cassette no longer puts out any film

Occasionally, you may wish to rewind a partially exposed roll of film, usually to replace it with a different type or ISO. To accomplish this, the IS-3 has a tiny REWIND button which is best activated with the tip of a ballpoint pen. The film will be rewound into the film cassette. If you wish to reload the partially exposed film back into the IS-3, film leader retrievers are available at most camera stores.

To reload a partially exposed film, switch on your IS-3 and set the exposure mode the Manual. Put the lens cap on the lens and press the PF button to disable the autofocus function. Now the IS-3 is ready for reloading. When 1 is displayed on the LCD, press the release until the counter indicates the frame number at which you removed the film from the IS-3 (hopefully, it was noted on the cassette). Press the release again twice more to make certain there is no overlap of frames. Press the MODE and +/- buttons simultaneously and return the camera controls to automatic if desired.

Film Advance

The film advance motor located in the rear of the camera receives commands in two ways:

One is by pressing the MODE and +/- buttons simultaneously, which returns the IS-3 to single frame advance, Program exposure mode and multi-zone metering. The S (SINGLE) in the lower part of the LCD panel indicates that the IS-3 will take only one exposure when the release is pressed. The camera will not fire, however, until the autofocus mechanism has locked onto a point of focus.

By using the DRIVE button, located below and to the left of the LCD panel and either of the switches marked SHIFT, additional film transport modes can be selected. Once a mode is selected. The DRIVE cycle consists of three transport modes, S - single frame advance, C - continuous film advance, and D.EXP - double-exposure mode. You must follow this progression through the DRIVE cycle each time the DRIVE button is pressed. The selected transport mode is indicated by blinking characters on the LCD.

Program Selection

Fifteen keys and buttons combine to control the IS-3's functions. These are located logically to follow functional requirements and for ease of use. The zoom buttons and the MACRO and PF buttons are on the front of the lens, the switch for the twin flash unit is next to the pop up unit, the power switch is located on the left of the body near the eyepiece (and hence always within the photographer's view). The four function buttons are located to the left and below the LCD panel. By activating the SHIFT buttons to the right of the LCD monitor and the SHIFT DIAL surrounding the shutter release you may use one of the four control buttons to send data and commands to the camera's CPU. This method of pushing and holding the button, selecting the function or fixing the data with the SHIFT controls is safety feature to prevent accidental setting or erasing of camera functions.

The MODE button is used to select the exposure program from among eight options.
The +/- button sets exposure corrections which are carried out only by activating

The DRIVE button is used to select the film advance modes.

The FLASH button selects one of three modes offered by the IS-3's twin flash unit.

Setting Modes and Functions

Set the desired operating mode and function by using the four buttons listed above then adjust the exposure correction factors either with the SHIFT control surrounding the shutter release or with the one next to the LCD monitor. The SHIFT control will move arrow-heads on the LCD panel to indicate the currently activated function.

To select the aperture use the SHIFT control while in exposure mode A - aperture priority or M - manual. To set the shutter speed, use the SHIFT dial surrounding the shutter release in modes S -shutter priority or M. None of these steps requires pressing another button.

By activating RESET with the MODE and +/- buttons the IS-3 is reset to the standard exposure program (leaving all other operating modes): automatic programming P with multi-zone metering ESP, single frame advance S, autofocus, AUTO or AUTO-S flash program; all correction factors are erased. Activation of the tiny rewind button on the camera's underside requires an extremely pointed object; a simple and reliable guarantee against accidental rewinding of the film.

The spot-metering button can be comfortably and conveniently reached by the right thumb when ones attention is on the image in the viewfinder.

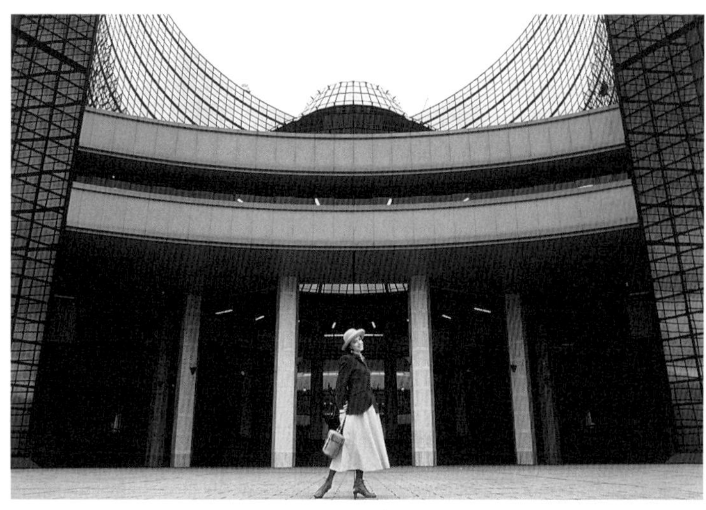

One way the IS-10 differs from the other IS cameras is an increased angle of view from 35mm (bottom) to 28mm (top).

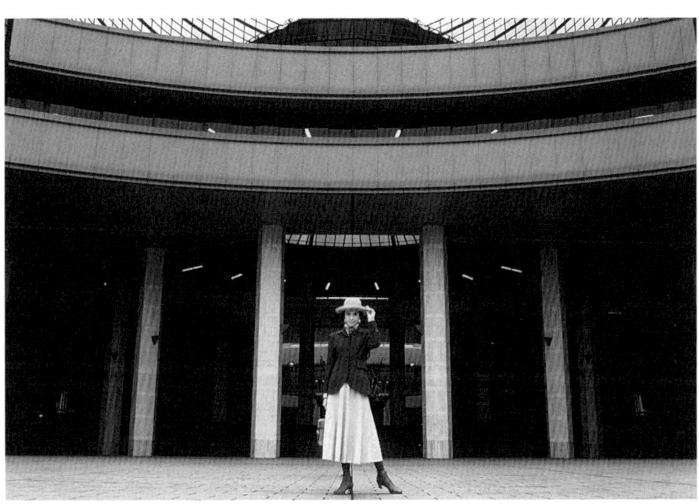

Using the IS-10

The new Olympus IS-10 is, at the same time, a continuation of the IS design philosophy and a radical departure from the previous IS series cameras. The IS-10 keeps the same general appearance and features, but does not use the S-curve film path used in the three original IS cameras, which makes it a bit wider than the other IS cameras, but does make film loading easier. It has a built in flash with only a single flash head, and does not have a flash shoe for the use of supplementary flash units. Instead of the large LCD panel on the camera back, the IS-10 has a rather small LCD panel to the right of the prism hump. Controls have been simplified as well, with a bi-directional, "FULL AUTO" button behind the shutter release button controlling all functions.

At the same time as this overall simplification, the IS-10 has been fitted with a very advanced 28-110mm zoom lens, which answers the criticism that the original IS cameras' zoom did not extend far enough into the wide angle range. Also added is a diopter setting for the eyepiece which allows you to adjust the camera's viewfinder precisely to your own vision.

Batteries

The Olympus IS-10 operates from two CR 123A Lithium batteries installed in a battery compartment on the bottom of the camera's integral hand grip. Every time the camera is switched on, it automatically tests the batteries and displays their condition with a symbol next to the frame counter on the LCD panel. When the image of a whole battery is shown in black, the batteries are good. When only half the battery is shown in black the batteries are beginning to fade and should be replaced shortly. When the battery is shown half black and flashes, the batteries must be replaced immediately.

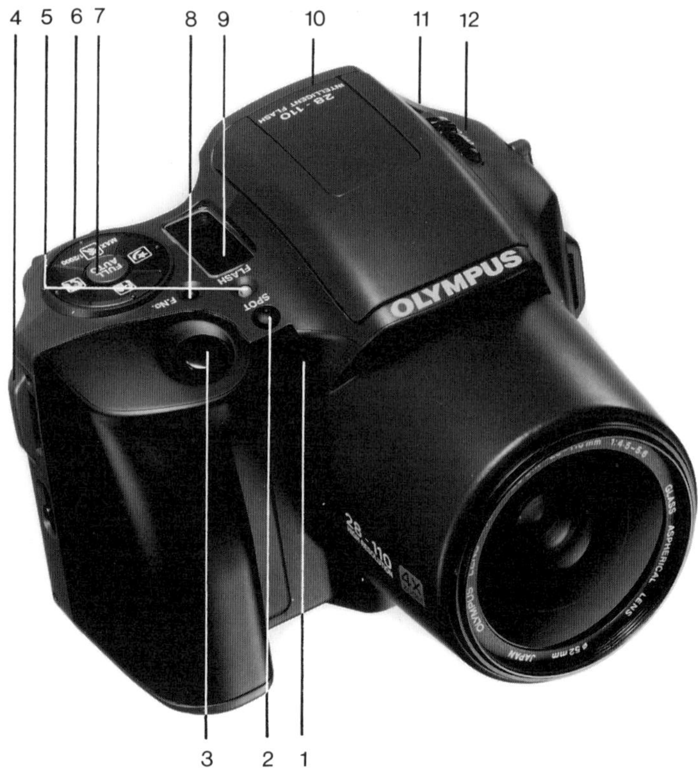

1. **Self-timer/remote control sensor**
2. **Spot button**
3. **Shutter release**
4. **Strap lug**
5. **Flash mode button**
6. **(on rear) Zoom buttons**
7. **Full Auto button**
8. **Aperture control button**
9. **LCD panel**
10. **Built-in flash**
11. **Self-timer/remote control button**
12. **Power switch/Flash release**

Camera Controls

Users of other IS cameras will have to make some adjustments when switching to the IS-10. The rocker switch which operates the power zoom is no longer on the left side of the zoom lens housing. It has been moved to the back of the camera, directly behind the shutter release button, and is now operated by the

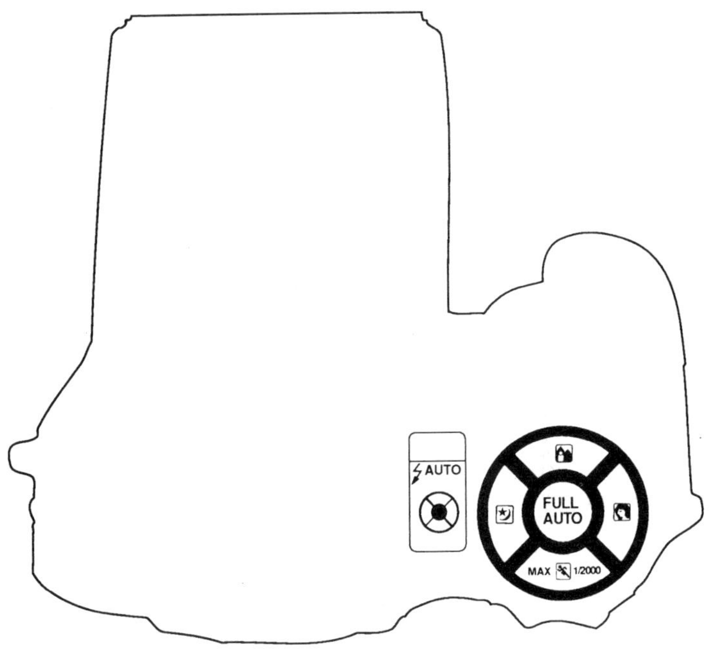

1. Full Auto button with Direct mode select buttons.
2. LCD panel

photographer's right thumb. Power zoom operation is smooth as on the other IS cameras, but on the IS-10 there is no way to switch the camera to manual focus. If the autofocus system can't achieve focus, you cannot take a picture. This limitation can be overcome by use of the focus lock, which activates with partial pressure on the shutter release button, and the selection of an alternate subject at the same distance as the desired subject. In operation, you let the camera focus on an alternate subject by gently pressing the shutter button until the in-focus indicator lights up. You then maintain pressure on the shutter release button, recompose, and without releasing the pressure, press the button all the way to take the picture.

If you wish to rewind the film before finishing a roll, a recessed black button on the camera bottom on the far left will activate the rewind sequence at any time. You will need to use a fingernail or ballpoint pen to press it.

Flash

The built-in flash has several operational modes which are controlled by pressing the small blue flash button just in front of the LCD panel. The normal mode is AUTO. In this mode, the flash will fire automatically when the camera's metering system senses that the light level is too low. Of course, if you do not want the flash to fire in a dim scene because you want a time exposure, you can turn the flash off by folding it back down. The second flash mode is AUTO-S. This is the red-eye reduction mode, and causes the flash to emit 20 preflashes prior to the flash which makes the exposure. The third mode is FILL-IN. This mode is for fill flash and causes the flash to fire every time regardless of light level.

Self-timer

The IS-10 has a 12 second self-timer delay. To the left of the camera's eyepiece is a blue button which controls both remote control and the self-timer. By pressing this button until the small clock face icon appears on the LCD panel, you can activate the self-timer. Pressing the shutter release button then locks the focus and exposure, and the camera will fire 12 seconds later.

Exposure Modes

Exposure modes on the IS-10 are basic and pictorial. The camera features four different subject-specific programs accessed by the "Full Auto" dial.

Sports/Action mode: indicated by an image of a runner, this sets the camera to favor faster shutter speeds for stopping action.

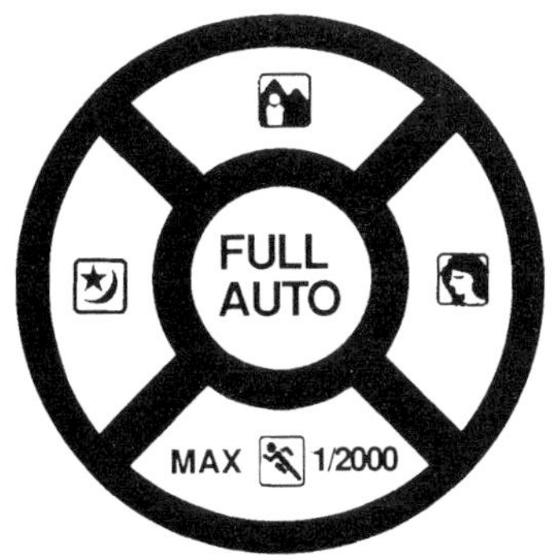

Full Auto button with Direct mode select buttons.

Portrait mode: indicated by a face icon, this mode is just the opposite and favors a wide aperture to blur out backgrounds. This emphasizes the portrait subject by separating it from the background.

Landscape mode: indicated by an image of a mountain with a person in front, it sets the camera for maximum depth of field.

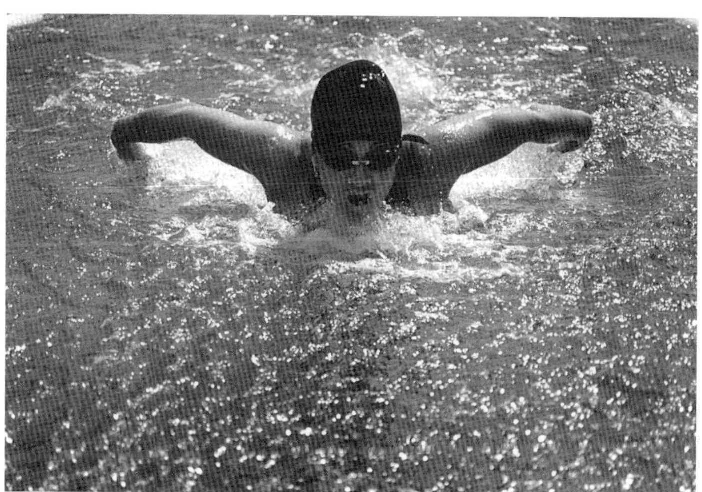

The Sports/Action program is made for photographs which require a fast shutter speed to stop the subject's motion.

Night scene mode: indicated by an image of a moon and star, this mode sets the camera for ambient exposure of backgrounds. You may place a subject in the foreground and use flash to illuminate this subject; both the subject and the background will be properly exposed. Because exposure times will be long, a tripod is necessary for this mode.

Aperture priority mode: If you want a bit more control, the IS-10 also offers aperture priority auto exposure. A small black button behind and to the left of the shutter release button is used to enter the desired aperture and the camera will then pick the appropriate shutter speed. The only limitation of this system is that you have no way of knowing what that shutter speed is, since there is no shutter speed readout on the camera. There is no way to manually select shutter speeds in any of the modes.

At any time and in any exposure mode it is possible to quickly switch back to a basic, fully automatic, programmed exposure mode by simply pressing the green button in the center of the main control switch array.

Spot meter

For backlighted subjects and other difficult exposure situations, the IS-10 offers a spot metering option. This is activated by pressing the small black button to the left of the shutter release button. Centered in the viewfinder is a circle which delineates the area from which the exposure reading is taken in spot metering mode.

To use the spot meter, choose an area as close to 18% gray as possible under the same lighting conditions as the subject. Fill the spot metering circle with the area and press the spot meter button. This takes the exposure reading from the area selected and locks it in so the picture can be recomposed. After you take the photograph, the spot metering function must be set again each time you wish to use it. Pressing the spot metering button before the exposure is made will disengage this option.

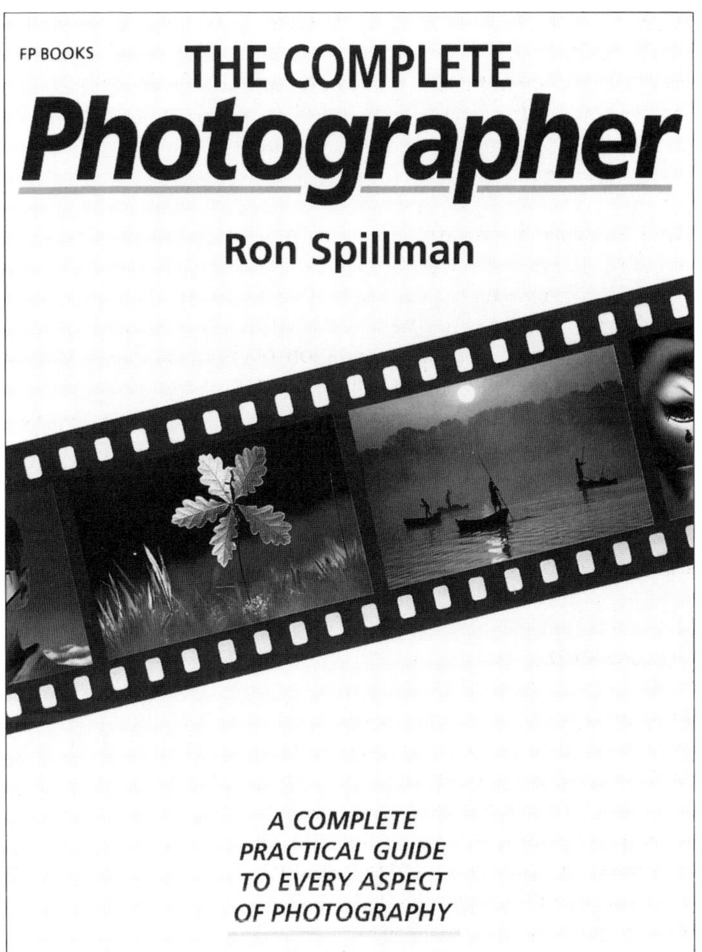

The Complete Photographer

by Ron Spillman

One of the most comprehensive general guides to photography available. This book covers everything the beginning or advanced photo enthusiast needs to know. Packed with invaluable tips, hints advice and information; illustrated with over 100 full-color photographs as well as instructional diagrams. Softcover. 192 pages.

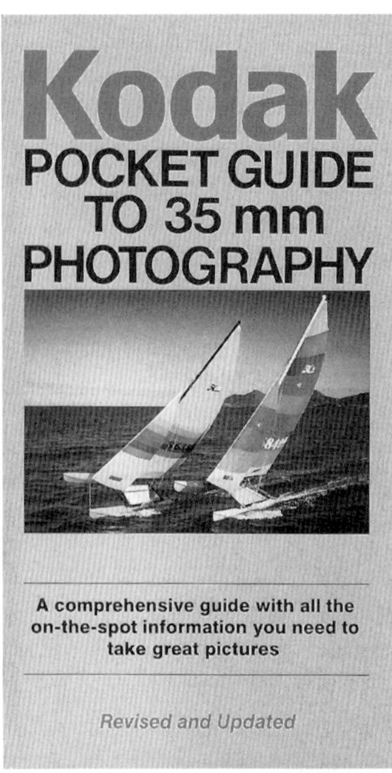

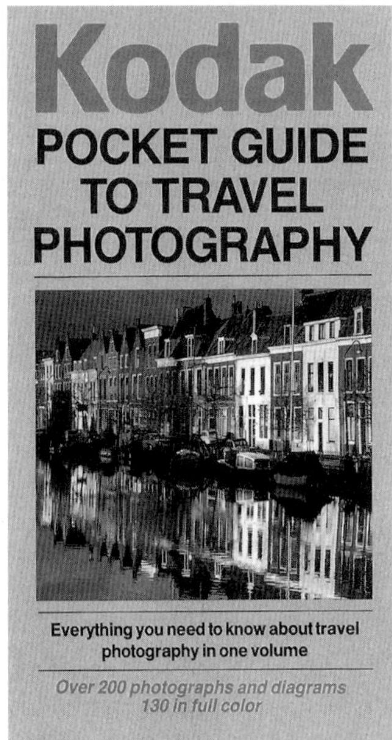

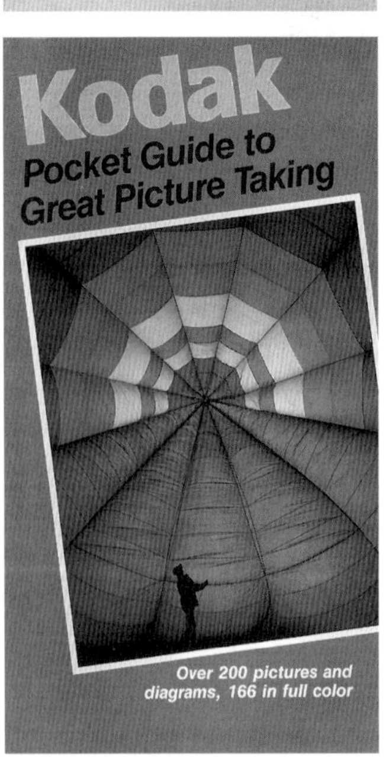

KODAK
Pocket Photo Guide Series

They may be pocket-sized but they are loaded with information and photos to give you on-the-spot advice on a variety of photo topics.

Notes

Notes

Notes

Notes

Notes